Library of
Davidson College

12: MONETARY REFORM AND WORLD INFLATION

THE WASHINGTON PAPERS
Volume I

12: MONETARY REFORM AND WORLD INFLATION

Robert Z. Aliber

THE CENTER FOR STRATEGIC AND INTERNATIONAL STUDIES
Georgetown University, Washington, D.C.

SAGE PUBLICATIONS
Beverly Hills / London

332.45
A 398 m

Copyright © 1973 by
The Center for Strategic and International Studies
Georgetown University

Printed in the United States of America

All rights reserved. No part of this book may be reproduced
or utilized in any form or by any means, electronic or mechanical,
including photocopying, recording, or by any
information storage and retrieval system, without permission in writing
from the publisher.

For information address:

SAGE PUBLICATIONS, INC.　　　　SAGE PUBLICATIONS LTD
275 South Beverly Drive　　　　　　　　　　　　St George's House / 44 Hatton Garden
Beverly Hills, California 90212　　　　　　　　London EC1N 8ER

International Standard Book Number 0-8039-0285-9

Library of Congress Catalog Card No. 73-86713

FIRST PRINTING

When citing a Washington Paper, please use the proper form. Remember to cite the series title and include the paper number. One of the two following formats can be adapted (depending on the style manual used):

(1) HASSNER, P. (1973) "Europe in the Age of Negotiation." The Washington Papers, I, 8. Beverly Hills and London: Sage Pubns.

OR

(2) Hassner, Pierre. 1973. *Europe in the Age of Negotiation.* The Washington Papers, vol. 1, no. 8. Beverly Hills and London: Sage Publications.

81-5448

CONTENTS

	Preface	1
I.	An Overview of the Monetary Reform Problem	9
II.	The Rise of the Dollar-Centered System	18
III.	The Management of the Dollar-Centered System	30
IV.	Monetary Reform as a Process	42
V.	The U.S. National Interests in International Monetary Reform	54
VI.	The U.S. National Interests and Alternative Monetary Arrangements	63
	Epilogue	77
	Notes	80
	References	82

AUTHOR'S NOTE: Fran Haydon, Annie Lowrey, and Ireta Stiger typed the several drafts of this essay during the summer of 1973. Charlie Aliber developed the tables. Christine Hekman, Richard M. Levich, and Ben Bachrach provided useful comments as the essay developed. I am grateful for their assistance.

PREFACE

A polite description of U.S. international monetary policy in the last decade is that it has been a costly disaster. This disaster had several causes—one was a confusion in the policy formation process between substantive objectives for U.S. economic policy and a formal objective. The formal objective, the avoidance of a change in the $35 price of gold, was pursued at considerable costs to substantive objectives like efficiency in the use of resources, government expenditures, foreign policy objectives, administrative effectiveness in the U.S. government, even, for a short while, full employment. But the $35 parity was changed, at first on an ad hoc basis by restricting U.S. payments abroad, and then in the latter half of 1971, on a formal basis by an increase in the dollar price of gold. The formal objective was not attained, yet the costs had been incurred. In retrospect, a broader view of alternatives available to the United States in the formation of international monetary policy might have led to a less costly policy.

Since 1971 the U.S. government has floundered in its attempt to formulate a new international monetary policy. And the difficulty reflects a confusion between the substantive objectives of U.S. policy and the mechanisms for achieving these objectives. One consequence has been the continued deterioration in U.S. economic relations with its major trading partners in the Atlantic system.[1]

International monetary policy is one of three major areas in which the United States has been in almost continual negotiations with other major industrial partners in the Atlantic system; the others are trade policy and security policy. These negotiations about trade and monetary issues reflect that the nation-state, even one as large and rich as the United States, is too small to secure economies of scale in production and the gains from trade. The negotiations about security reflect that a collective or at least coordinated defense policy is much less expensive than individual national policies; indeed such policies are simply not feasible for smaller countries. And the U.S. interest in security arrangements with friendly countries is to gain their cooperation in expenditures, manpower, bases, and strategy. Trade policy has been successful, as evidenced by the reduction in barriers to the movement of goods. And security policy also has been successful for there has been no major war and the costs to the United States of maintaining its military security have been lower.

Despite the weblike relationship among security, trade, and money, monetary policy is at a somewhat lower level than security and trade in the hierarchy of U.S. national objectives. Security is the ultimate objective, for it is essential for the preservation of free institutions; economic welfare, which is what the trade issues are about, is somewhat less important. Both security and trade policies have obvious profound implications for political and economic welfare. But monetary policy, in contrast, has no direct welfare connotations; rather monetary policy and the monetary mechanism are tools or instruments that provide a framework that may facilitate—or handicap—the attainment of the security and trade objectives.

The effort and energy expended on the maintenance of the $35 parity have compromised the attainment of U.S. objectives for trade policy and security policy. Whereas an efficient international monetary policy should make it easier to attain these U.S. objectives, the misplaced focus of U.S. international monetary policy has meant that trade and security policies have been compromised as the United States has sought concessions from other Atlantic nations in the trade and security issues to help retain the $35 parity.

Even with the most successful of international monetary policies, changes in the exchange rates and in the dollar price of gold were inevitable—given the monetary policies in the United States and other Atlantic nations, and the consequent movements in the domestic price levels in these countries. Monetary relations among the Atlantic nations have been in disarray for more than a decade, initially in anticipation of the inevitable change in the dollar price of gold and subsequently in anticipation of the need to revamp the exchange rate structure. The private demand for gold began to increase in the mid-1960s partially in anticipation of an increase in the monetary price of gold. The attempt to avoid a change in the dollar price of gold became mixed up with the exchange rate misalignment in the late 1960s. Both the undervaluation of gold and the overvaluation of the dollar led to a massive flight by private investors from the dollar in 1969, 1970, and 1971. These investors sold $50 billion of assets denominated in dollars to buy assets denominated in German marks, Swiss francs, Japanese yen, and other currencies. Foreign central banks acquired $50 billion of dollar-denominated assets. This run on the dollar continued at a lesser pace in 1972. With the move to floating exchange rates in February 1973, the run on the dollar continued; the dollar depreciated in the exchange market more sharply than would have been predicted from changes in fundamental economic relationships between the United States and the other Atlantic nations. This flight from the dollar was symptomatic both of the turmoil and instability in monetary relationships and of shaken investor confidence in U.S. leadership in international monetary policy.

Both the breakdown in the exchange rate system and the flight from the dollar were triggered by worldwide inflation, which received its initial stimulus from the U.S. policies for financing the Vietnam War. Whereas the United States was the price stability leader in the 1955-1965 period, the U.S. commodity level price began to rise at a more rapid rate in 1966 and 1967 than commodity price levels in other Atlantic nations. A change in the levels exchange rate structure appeared inevitable as a result of these differentials in rates of price increase at about the same time as a change in the monetary price of gold was necessary because of a global gold shortage.

The sequence of monetary events since 1970 has indicated the disarray in the system—countries shifted between pegged and floating rates, adoped multiple exchange rate practices, and intensified their controls on international payments, and even applied these controls in a discriminatory fashion. Gold was demonetized, at least temporarily; its monetary future was clouded. The inevitable changes in the exchange rate structure associated with the Vietnam War inflation had occurred by the end of 1971; the anticipated stability was not realized, in part because of a surge in the U.S. inflation rate. And the resulting problem was how international monetary stability might be achieved while the rate of U.S. domestic inflation was high.

Now, after the international monetary turmoil of the last five years, the recognized need is to reestablish more orderly international monetary arrangements—to establish a set of arrangements so businessmen can have greater confidence in the levels of exchange rates and exchange controls, and so central bankers in various countries can have greater confidence in the international monetary policies that their trading partners might adopt. Reestablishing order involves more than signing a treaty binding the Atlantic nations to follow certain policies regarding exchange market intervention and the use of gold and the dollar as international reserve assets. A necessary condition for international monetary order is that the United States achieve stability in its domestic price and employment policies: revamping of the international monetary arrangements, however far-reaching, will have a minimal impact in the absence of stability in the underlying economic structure. But stability in U.S. prices and employment alone is not sufficient for order in the international monetary system; rather the exchange rate policies and the structure of international reserve arrangements must be consistent with each other and consistent with the mix of national monetary policies.

The problems of the international monetary system over the last decade have stimulated extensive research. The direct usefulness of much of the materials to the formation of policy is questionable, and for two reasons. The first is that much of the discussion is apolitical; the diversity in national interests among the Atlantic nations is not recognized explicitly. Thus the behavioral patterns and preferences of central banks in various countries have been generally ignored; implicity, it has been assumed that these central banks in various countries would adjust their preferences to suit the characteristics of the international system—or the desire of the U.S. authorities to avoid a change in the dollar price of gold. It was unclear how the national interests of various countries would be served if each of the proposals had been implemented. The second is that the proposals for reform of the system were generally advanced without explicit comparison with the merits and the costs of the alternatives; each expert favored his own proposal, which was usually advanced as if its superiority to competing proposals would be self-evident.

In the last decade I have tried to evaluate the costs and benefits to the United States of several of the major alternatives to the then-current arrangements. Several assumptions were implicit in this approach. One was that U.S. national interests and those of other countries diverge. A second was that the problem of defining the cosmopolitan interest was so difficult that it seemed more productive to focus on promoting the U.S. national interests, the belief being that U.S. foreign policy interests would incorporate the national interests of other countries.

The Future of the Dollar as an International Currency (Aliber: 1966), written in 1964 when a change in the dollar price of gold appeared inevitable, but before the U.S. inflation had surged and the need for changes in exchange rates became evident, discussed how the international roles of the dollar would be affected if the dollar were no longer convertible into gold at $35. One alternative was that other currencies might float in terms of the dollar, a second was a uniform increase in the monetary price of gold. One theme was that the international roles of the dollar had developed in response to demands of other countries for an asset to fill several functions, and that the dollar satisfied these diverse demands better than other assets did. These roles for the dollar would be largely unchanged if the international monetary arrangements were changed. The argument was that the international roles of the dollar reflected basic economic forces in the world, such as the economic strength of the U.S. economy and its openness, and not the international monetary arrangements centered on the $35 parity. Thus, while certain costs associated with a move from the $35 parity would be one-shot and associated with the transition to a new arrangement; it was argued that it was preferable to incur the costs rather than to incur costs of maintaining the parity.

Choices for the Dollar (1969) was written in the latter months of 1968, when it seemed that a change in the exchange rate structure was inevitable. The purpose was to assess whether the U.S. interests would be better served by one of the alternatives to the $35 parity: a small devaluation to $42, a worldwide increase in the monetary price of gold, or demonetization of gold.

By accident rather than by plan, this essay is thus the third in a sequence. Once again an attempt is made to define how the U.S. national interests might be served by various alternatives to the current arrangement. Reform is necessary to restore order and stability in the international system—and the process of reform must recognize the built-in imbalances that are left from the breakdown in previous arrangements. The Bretton Woods system has completely collapsed, the dollar has lost its luster as a reserve asset, and the Atlantic nations are subject to more persistent inflation than at any time since World War II.

This essay has several themes. One is that changes in international monetary arrangements must "fit" or be consistent with the structural economic relationships among the Atlantic nations. One implication of this theme is that if international monetary reform should lead to an arrangement that is not harmonious with the underlying economic relationships, that arrangement will prove a charade and soon falter. In the long run, market forces dominate, and the institutional arrangements must be consistent with these forces. A second theme is that conflicts of interest between the United States and other Atlantic countries on international monetary reform result from their concern over economic welfare and political advantages, and so monetary reform should be considered an exercise in U.S. foreign policy.

The remainder of this essay is divided into six sections. The next section traces the sources of instability in the international system and the need for reform. Section II discusses the development of the international monetary system over the last half-century, and the contrast between the economic structure of the system and the formal or institutional arrangements. Section III deals with the breakdown of the international system, including the inability of a given set of institutional arrangements to adapt to developments in a non-inflationary environment and then in an inflationary environment. The fourth section deals with the process of international monetary reform; reform is essentially a rule-making exercise. The fifth section analyzes the U.S. national interests in international monetary reform, while the final section evaluates how these interests might be served under alternative arrangements.

I.

An Overview of the Monetary Reform Problem

The last several years have been difficult for the United States in international monetary policy. In August 1971, the Nixon Administration announced that the U.S. Treasury would no longer sell gold to foreign central banks in exchange for dollars at the rate of $35 an ounce, as it had since 1934. The then Secretary of the Treasury, John Connally, denied that the dollar would be devalued. At the end of 1971, as part of the Smithsonian Agreement—hailed by President Nixon as "the greatest monetary agreement in history"—the dollar price of gold was increased to $38 while the currencies of other Atlantic countries were revalued relative to the dollar. The U.S. payments deficit in 1971 was the largest that one country—or indeed any group of countries—had incurred in any one year; foreign central banks added $30 billion of dollar assets to their holdings of reserves.

During 1972, as foreign central banks were acquiring billions more of dollar assets, it became clear that the Smithsonian Agreement had failed to staunch the U.S. payments deficit. In February 1973, a new exchange crisis, centered on the dollar, erupted; and the Smithsonian Agreement broke down. Other Atlantic nations permitted their currencies to float in the exchange market, and most appreciated relative to the dollar. While the dollar price of gold was increased to $42, foreign central banks could not buy gold from the U.S. Treasury.

These changes in exchange rates and gold market arrangements mean that the rules of the International Monetary Fund are obsolete. The Fund remains modestly active (international institutions never die, even though their original justifications do) but the Fund's articles and rules are now largely irrelevant. Foreign central banks hold a larger volume of dollar assets than they prefer. The usefulness of gold holdings of foreign central banks in monetary settlements is questionable. Perhaps more importantly, the consensus among Atlantic nations on how the international system should operate has been shattered.

The international monetary system—by definition—is a set of arrangements for integrating separate national monetary systems.[2] The international system is subject to two countervailing forces. The demand for efficiency in international transactions tends to reduce the importance of the distinctions among national currencies, so that international transactions are minimally more difficult than domestic transactions; this is the centralizing tendency. A decentralizing tendency results when individual countries want to follow the monetary and fiscal policies they believe appropriate for their national economic interests—and the future price relationship among national currencies may differ from the current one as a consequence of these policies. If the centralizing pulls are dominant, then the pursuit of national economic interests becomes subordinate to efficiency in international trade and payments. In contrast, if the decentralizing pulls are dominant, the costs of various international transactions rise relative to the costs of domestic transactions because the lack of harmonization of national economic policies may lead to sharp changes in the exchange rates and in exchange controls—and the anticipation of such changes may lead to considerable uncertainty before the event about whether these changes will occur.

Economic efficiency pulls in the direction of consolidation, while economic nationalism pulls in the direction of fragmentation. The design and the operation of the international financial system concern the appropriate balance between these two divergent pulls. And as long as there is an international system—as long as there are national economies with separate monies and divergent economic interests—these two forces pull against each other. The appropriate balance between these pulls shifts through time in response to changing economic forces and changing nationalist sentiments within individual countries.

Permitting individual countries to follow the monetary and fiscal policies they deem best for their national interests would be of limited concern in a world of isolated economies, for these policies would have no impact on the performance and policies of other countries. But few economies are isolated. Each country's monetary and fiscal policies affect its trade and payments balances. And each country's trade and payments balances are related to those of other countries. Moreover, individual countries may have targets for these balances that are inconsistent. In some cases, a country's trade balance target or its payments balance target may reflect that it wants to add to its holdings of international reserve assets. No major problems arise as long as the targeted levels for the payments surpluses and the trade surpluses are consistent with each other. But frequently the targets are globally inconsistent. Japan may want a payments surplus of $2 billion and France one of $1 billion, when other countries, as a group, also want to be in payments surplus. On a worldwide basis the target payments surpluses and hence the target rate of growth of demand for international reserves exceed the rate of growth of the supply of reserves; some mechanism is needed to reconcile the inconsistency.

Some countries want to achieve trade surpluses because of the expansive effect on their domestic employment levels, while others may want to avoid large trade surpluses because of their inflationary impact on their commodity price levels. And so the desired trade balances of these countries must be consistent with their target levels of employment; every country, however, cannot simultaneously run a trade surplus as a way of increasing domestic employment. Nor can every country simultaneously run a trade deficit to reduce the upward pressure on domestic price levels.

One solution for the consistency problem, given the framework of institutional arrangements, is to induce various countries to change their domestic economic policies so national policies are consistent. Another is to change the institutional arrangements, perhaps by adjusting the rate of growth of international reserves, or the exchange rate alignment, or even the system of exchange rates. And both national policies and institutional arrangements could be changed together. Yet changes in the framework, however far-reaching, may prove insufficient to resolve all of the inconsistencies among national economic policies.

Inconsistency in National Policies

The inconsistency between the demand for and supply of international reserves in the 1960s led to numerous proposals for reform of the international monetary system. And the growing inconsistencies between U.S. economic policies and those of the other Atlantic nations in 1970 and 1971 led to proposals for changing both the exchange rates and the exchange rate system. The United States favored a change in exchange rates to disengage the U.S. economy from the mercantilist policies of other Atlantic nations—from their desires to achieve large trade surpluses, especially when they had domestic recessions. The policy makers in these other countries were ambivalent; they favored decreases in their trade surpluses as a way to reduce the inflationary pressures on their domestic price levels. But at the same time they were reluctant to accept the declines in their trade surpluses because of the adverse impacts on both their domestic levels of employment as well as on profits in their exporting and import competing industries.

One generally accepted way to reduce the trade imbalances involved a reduction in the price of the dollar relative to the currencies of other Atlantic countries. But even where there was an agreement on this policy, the United States and other Atlantic countries disagreed both on where the initiative for the change should come from and how large a change in the exchange rates was needed. Americans wanted other countries to revalue their currencies in terms of gold and the dollar; so that the $35 parity might be retained. Other countries favored an increase in the dollar price of gold to minimize the domestic political costs and the decline in the domestic currency value of the international reserve assets.[3] The United States sought to reduce the deficit in its international payments by about $9 billion a year while the surplus countries were willing only to accept reductions in their surpluses totalling $3 billion.

Eventually, after six months of bargaining and indecision, a compromise was reached: the United States raised the dollar price of gold by about 10 percent. As a group, other Atlantic countries revalued their currencies relative to the dollar by an average of about 12 percent. But this change proved inadequate to reduce the sharp imbalances in international payments in 1972, and speculation against the dollar again became intense in late 1972 and early 1973.

After the February 1973 exchange crises, continued reliance on the pegged exchange rate system was impracticable, because investors no longer had confidence in the ability of central bankers to set the appropriate exchange rates. Hence a move to floating rates was inevitable; in effect there was no viable alternative.

The floating rate system was expected to bring the stability to the exchange market that had disappeared under the pegged rate system; the price of the dollar in terms of currencies of other Atlantic countries could move continuously in response to market forces and by relatively small amounts. Yet the sharp movements in the foreign exchange value of the dollar in terms of the mark, the Swiss franc, and other currencies under the floating rate system demonstrated that the instability was in the economic policies of the Atlantic nations, not in the exchange rate system.

For more than five months after the adoption of a floating rate system, the value of the dollar in marks, Swiss francs, and other currencies continued to decline. The depreciation of the dollar in the foreign exchange market was viewed as an external reflection of the decline in its value in domestic commodity markets. Between 1967 and 1972, the U.S. price level increased by more than 30 percent. Some observers saw no end to the decline in the foreign exchange value of the dollar, in part, apparently, because they expected U.S. commodity prices to rise at the rate of 5, 6, or 7 percent a year.

The puzzling phenomenon in 1973 was that the dollar continued to decline in value in the exchange market, even though prices abroad, as measured by the consumer price indices, were rising at least as rapidly as in the United States. There were numerous ad hoc and nonprice explanations for the weakness of the dollar in the exchange market: Watergate and the decline in confidence in U.S. leadership; the energy crisis and the increase in U.S. imports of petroleum; the activities of multinational firms in shifting production to lower-cost foreign centers; and the increase in productivity abroad in traditional industries and the decline in the U.S. technological lead.

Altogether the scope, duration, and persistence of the 1970s inflation is unprecedented in the twentieth century—except during the World Wars I and II. During the Korean War period, U.S. consumer prices increased by about 10 percent over a two-year period; by 1953, the inflationary episode was over, and the rate of annual price increase was less than 1 percent. The current inflation, however, has persisted since 1966, and the annual rate of price increase has varied between 3 and 6 percent. The continuation of the inflation, long after the Vietnam War was wound down, and indeed the increase in the annual rate of price increase in 1972 and 1973, suggests there have been some important changes in economic structure.

The breakdown of the Bretton Woods monetary arrangements during this worldwide inflationary episode was predictable, for they were designed to cope with a depression in the world economy, not with a worldwide inflation. And these arrangements were designed to deal with devaluations of other currencies relative to the dollar, rather than with the devaluation of the dollar.

Divergent Interests and Monetary Reform

For much of the last decade, economists and government officials have focused their attention on modifying the existing arrangements for financing imbalances and for handling changes in exchange rates. Today's renewed interest comes on top of the numerous changes that have been made since Bretton Woods, including the gold pool, the General Arrangements to Borrow, and the increases in member-country quotas in the International Monetary Fund in 1964 and 1968. In 1968, establishment of the Special Drawing Rights (SDRs) arrangement, which involved the production of a new international money, was a major change. Ministers of Finance appeared to have been in almost continuous negotiation in the late 1960s.

Several factors explain why the extensive negotiations about reform did not result in a stable monetary arrangement. In part, changes in these institutional arrangements were viewed as ends in themselves; the focus was on consistency in the payments balances of Atlantic countries. Relatively little attention was given to measures that might facilitate consistency among national monetary and fiscal policies. Moreover, the fragmentation tendencies were ascendant; within nearly every country, nationalist sentiments were becoming stronger. Finally, the nature of the international financial problem has changed over the decade. Initially the problem centered on the inadequate growth of international reserves, then it became the overvaluation of the dollar, and then the breakdown in the pegged exchange rate system. Despite the accomplishments of the last decade, international monetary reform is now more urgent, for the previous negotiations were patchwork measures designed to facilitate retention of the $35 parity, whereas now the problem is to develop a stable and open system.

Negotiations of the last decade were nearly all a response to U.S. contentions: that there was a shortage of gold and a shortage of international money, and then, subsequently, that the exchange rate structure was too rigid. The American view was that the persistent U.S. payments deficit was a system problem, not a country (meaning the United States) problem. And this view was tenable until the mid-1960s. But many other Atlantic countries, especially France, refused to accept this explanation or accepted it only grudgingly. They believed—or at least they argued—that if the United States followed the "right" domestic policies, the system's problems would disappear. And their argument was formally correct in that sufficiently severe deflationary U.S.

monetary policies would force world prices down to the level at which the supply of reserves would be adequate to satisfy the demand without a U.S. payments deficit. Revamping the monetary arrangements so the growth in the supply of reserves would be more rapid, and hence able to meet the demand, appeared a less costly approach toward consistency.

Earlier in the postwar period, other Atlantic countries acquiesced in the U.S. initiatives to change monetary arrangements, unless there was strong indication that the proposed arrangement would adversely affect their own interests. The IMF arrangement was basically a U.S. proposal. Other countries tended to accept the U.S. initiatives because the net balance of "favors" had been so strongly on the side of the United States. The United States provided an umbrella for international monetary arrangements; few costs were attached to following U.S. leadership.

The power relationships among Atlantic nations now differ from those in the early postwar period. Accepting the U.S. proposals for international monetary reform is now viewed as more costly to the other Atlantic nations. They feel, now that their economies are prosperous, and that there is some measure of economic integration in Europe, that they are in a stronger position to reject those U.S. initiatives which they believe might be costly to their interests. The net balance of "favors" is now less of the U.S. side because of measures taken by others in "Defense of the Dollar." Gaining their assent to U.S. proposals is now less easy.

In a formal sense, the breakdown in the system was initiated by the unilateral abrogation by the United States of its Bretton Woods treaty commitments. But even before August 1971, the development of the massive imbalance, and the unwillingness of the United States to devalue the dollar in terms of gold or of the Europeans and the Japanese to revalue their currencies, reflected a breakdown in communications among the Atlantic countries. That the negotiations about reform since then have proved so slow has been disheartening, and the consequence is that the United States and the other Atlantic nations have come to distrust each other's motives in the negotiations. These suspicions, more emotional than rational, are variations on the themes of "the Europeans are out to screw us" or "they want us over the barrel" or "they want to prolong the free ride" from the U.S. authorities. The Americans are not alone, however, for the Europeans complain that "they want to dump their fiscal problems in our laps," and "the Americans lack monetary discipline."

Slogans are not a substitute for policy. Policy involves identifying objectives, and then determining the low-cost way to achieve these objectives. The U.S. objectives are not fully consistent with those of other Atlantic countries, although there is substantial overlap. Moreover, monetary reform does not occur in a historical vacuum; the new arrangements must recognize that central banks hold $50 billion of gold and $70 billion of U.S. dollar-denominated assets. Finally monetary reform must implicitly recognize the confidence and trust that each of the Atlantic nations will place in the commitments of others.

The economic issues in monetary reform involve defining the feasible or workable set of institutional arrangements; feasibility is determined by the test of consistency. The components in the international system must be consistent with each other, and with the domestic economic policies of the several countries.

Political considerations further narrow the possible choice, since what is economically feasible may not be politically desirable. And what is politically desirable is determined by a rather rough matching of the perceived costs and benefits of the new arrangements to the participating countries.

The United States can seek to persuade the other Atlantic countries to accept the U.S. view, which may incur some costs, or else the United States can accept the European view, which also incurs costs. So a rather complicated calculus is needed to determine whether the costs of achieving U.S. objectives by persuasion are higher or lower than the costs of accepting the European view.

II.

The Rise of the Dollar-Centered System

One of the apparent paradoxes in the international system has been the large volume of dollar-denominated assets held by foreign central banks and other foreigners and the rapid growth in these holdings, at a time when the dollar was said to be weak. At the end of 1973, foreign central banks and monetary institutions held $70 billion of international reserve assets denominated in dollars, and foreign private parties held $60 billion of short-term dollar-denominated assets. The dollar holdings of these non-official foreigners were at their own choice; none was obliged to hold dollar assets. While the dollar holdings of some central banks were larger than they preferred, no foreign central bank had been obliged to acquire these dollar assets; each preferred to increase its holdings of these assets rather than take measures to prevent such an increase. And that the holdings in dollars were so very much larger than similar holdings denominated in sterling, German marks, Swiss francs, Japanese yen—individually or as a group—indicates the central role of the dollar in the international system during the last decades.

The eminent position of the dollar in the international system is a relatively recent phenomenon. One hundred years ago, the dollar was in the second or third rank of national currencies. The United States still had not yet established a central bank. Partly as a consequence, financial crises occurred about once a decade. The dollar had been floating since 1863 relative to sterling and gold; not until 1878 did the United States again peg the dollar to gold, in effect restoring a pegged exchange rate arrangement. The period of floating exchange rates was an adjustment to the inflationary U.S. financial policies pursued during the Civil War: between 1860 and 1865 the U.S. commodity price level doubled. The deflation of 1865-1878 enabled the United States to repeg the dollar to gold at its pre-Civil War parity. While the dollar was pegged to gold for the forty-year period prior to U.S. entry into World War I in 1918, the dollar was still very much in the second rank of national currencies.

Within the thirty-year interval from the beginning of World War I to the end of World War II, the dollar had become the major international currency. Few national monies ever obtain the status of international monies; most national monies are used almost exclusively for payments among residents of the same country. To say the dollar is an international money is to say it has been used for payments among residents of different countries, both between U.S. residents and foreign residents, and between residents of different foreign countries. The dollar's role as the principal international money was the result of the desire of central banks and other investors to reduce the costs and uncertainty of their transactions and investments. These economic agents—governments, business firms, private individuals—acted in their own economic self-interest; they believed they would enhance their own welfare by holding dollar-denominated assets.

The analogy with the development of national monies may provide some insight into the development of an international money. In the absence of monies, transactions between individuals, even in the same country, involve barter. But barter is inconvenient for several reasons. The units to be exchanged may not be readily divisible, and so they may not match in value. There is no ready way to compare prices of different goods at the same time nor of the same good over time. And so economic agents found it useful to select one good or asset that was desirable for its own sake and, as well, might facilitate transactions in other goods. This asset is thus termed an "intermediate asset." The intermediate asset had to have qualities or attributes that other assets lacked: it had to be homogenous, readily divisible, and easily stored; it also had to have stability in value in relation to a wide array of other assets. Numerous assets might have satisfied these needs, some better than others. And the asset that best satisfied these needs became the money. Barter became obsolete because it was less efficient.

Because gold was used as the money, economic agents held more gold than they would have if gold had been only a commodity. Costs were attached to these holdings, otherwise the wealth invested in money might be invested in other ways. Yet economic agents incurred these costs—which were avoidable under a barter system—because of the greater efficiency in the use of money.

One important characteristic of money was that it served as the numeraire; the values of all other assets are expressed in terms of units of the numeraire. But an asset would only be used as the numeraire if it maintained its own value over time relative to a wide array of other assets; once its value began to change over time, its usefulness as numeraire declined. And the search for a new numeraire would begin.

Textbooks in economics typically describe the three uses of money as a medium of payment, a unit-of-account, and a store of value. Some assets satisfy these attributes better than others. Thus houses and life insurance policies may be effective stores of value, while green stamps and subway tokens are mediums of payment. But life insurance policies are not very good as a medium of payment, and subway tokens are an inconvenient way to store wealth. Numerous assets have been used as money. "Competition" among the assets has greatly reduced the number of monies, and those that are still used as money have a more attractive set of attributes than those no longer used.

Gold was used as a money for an extended period and was an international money, since payments in gold were acceptable in many countries. Gold was the numeraire, since prices were expressed in units of gold. While each country might have its own unit-of-account, the values of coin issued in different countries could be readily compared by their gold values. While silver, copper, and other commodities have also been used as monies at the same time as gold, their monetary roles have been gradually displaced. The decline in the number of commodity monies reflected the inconvenience and the uncertainties of retaining two commodity monies in the system.

Just as economic forces led to the consolidation in the number of commodity monies, so they led to increased use of dollar assets rather than gold as an international money. Some non-U.S. resident holders of gold began to find that holdings of dollar-denominated assets better suited their needs than holdings of gold. That the international role of the dollar increased relative to the international role of gold was a result of market forces. Much as gold eventually displaced silver from the monetary system, so the dollar began to displace gold in certain international roles.

Several stages are evident in the competitive process as one money displaces another. The growth of national monies initially depended on the willingness of the national central banks to convert liabilities denominated in their currencies into gold on demand. Without this commitment, investors would not have held the national monies, since in the long run they might prove less valuable than gold. While national monies might be preferred for convenience, the benefit of the convenience factor of national monies might be dominated by the uncertainty about their future value. And so central banks committed themselves to exchange national monies into gold to provide confidence about their future value.

The Dollar As International Money

World War I gave a strong stimulus to the growth of the dollar as an international money. The war in Europe started in 1913; the United States formally entered the war toward the end of 1918. Whereas the European central banks ceased converting their currencies into gold when the war started, the dollar remained convertible into gold. Moreover, because of the submarine scare, gold shipments were embargoed. The policies adopted to finance the war were usually inflationary, but the price increases in Europe were much greater than in the United States. The United States became a source of supply to European belligerents; U.S. exports increased sharply relative to U.S. imports. This export surplus was financed in part by sales of gold by foreign institutions to the United States. These governments also tended to sell their holdings—requisitioned from their nationals—of U.S. securities. Some European governments, especially Great Britain, borrowed extensively from U.S. investors to get the dollars to finance their U.S. purchases; and, after U.S. entry in the war, they borrowed from the U.S. government. European central banks began to hold the receipts from their security sales as dollar deposits, boosting the role of the dollar as a reserve asset.

For many countries, one advantage of holding dollar-denominated assets was that the risk of loss from changes in the price of their reserves relative to the price of their imports was smaller, since a substantial part of their imports came from the United States. And the United States had been more effective in achieving stable prices than any other major country.

The dollar became the numeraire for the system not because of any treaty or agreement, but because various countries had decided, in their own self-interest, to peg their currencies to the dollar. U.S. policies toward its own price level had a major impact on the world price level, because so many countries pegged their currencies to the dollar. Even while gold was still used as a reserve asset, its role as numeraire was displaced by the dollar, since the changes in the U.S. price level were increasingly independent of changes in U.S. gold holdings. The world began to move on to a dollar standard much as, at an earlier period, the world had been on a gold standard. Yet gold was retained in the system. Some countries had a strong historical tie to gold; they wanted to hold all of their reserves in gold, because they viewed these holdings as less risky than the alternatives.

The events of the immediate postwar years strengthened the dollar's standing as an international currency. The European currencies were floating, and they depreciated sharply. Because only the dollar remained convertible into gold, newly produced gold flowed to the United States. U.S. monetary policy was directed toward achieving price stability, whereas monetary policy in Europe generally was deflationary. The United States enjoyed a general economic boom; whereas Europe tended to stagnate because of the deflationary monetary policy. But there were exceptions; several European currencies were subject to extensive inflation, and their currencies eventually became worthless; this happened in Austria and Germany. And political instability in Europe, in both France and Germany, tended to strengthen investor demand for assets denominated in other currencies.

By the middle of the 1920s, most of the European countries had again pegged their currencies to gold. Several had been pegged at their prewar parities. Most, however, had new parities; in effect they devalued their currencies relative to the dollar during the 1913-1925 period. Yet the pattern of the exchange rates that had been established by the mid-1920s—a pattern that resulted from the separate decision of each country about the best level for its own gold parity—was inconsistent with each other when viewed in the global context. Sterling was overvalued, while the French franc and the Belgian franc were undervalued. The British authorities faced the problem of how to maintain an overvalued parity. British interest rates were higher than desirable for domestic reasons, thus unemployment was severe. The British authorities asked the U.S. authorities to keep U.S. interest rates low to reduce the pull of funds from London to New York. The British also prevailed upon the French authorities, who owned large sterling deposits, not to buy gold from the Bank of England.

The 1930s was a decade of turmoil in international finance, partly the external reflection of the turmoil in the domestic economies. Because the unemployment and price-level variations in the 1930s were more severe in the United States than in other Atlantic nations, the international position of the dollar might have slipped. Two factors, however, produced the opposite result. One was the sharp increase in the dollar price of gold in 1934. A change in the dollar price of gold was inevitable, because gold was flowing from the United States in response to an expectation of a change in U.S. gold parity. But it was not inevitable that the United States would increase the dollar price of gold by 75 percent—from $20.67 an ounce to $35.00 an ounce. The rationale for this sharp increase was the anticipation that it would pull the United States out of the Great Depression. The international consequence was that the dollar was substantially undervalued relative to the currencies of other Atlantic nations. Other countries were then obliged to increase the price of gold in terms of their currencies. As a result, the worldwide monetary price of gold nearly doubled, but more by accident than by intent. Gold production was stimulated, while the private demand for gold fell. A gold glut resulted. Much of the excess gold came to the United States, and it had the effect of strengthening the position of the dollar.

The second factor was the growing threat of war in Europe, which meant that the United States seemed an increasingly attractive haven for wealth. And so Europeans began to acquire various types of dollar securities. The threat to the stability of European currencies—the association of wars with exchange controls and inflation—reduced the attractiveness of currencies of other Atlantic countries relative to the dollar.

World War II had consequences for the dollar much like World War I. The war in Europe began more than two years before the United States entered as a belligerent. During this interval the United States became a source of supply for the rest of the world, the U.S. trade balance improved sharply, and the United States became a sizeable lender to other countries. Gold, both newly produced and from private and public holdings, flowed to the United States. By the end of the war, the U.S. Treasury held more than 75 percent of the total world monetary gold. While World War II was less inflationary than World War I for all participants, the United States experienced less rapid inflation than did the European countries.

World War II was much more destructive than World War I, in terms of plant, equipment, infrastructure, and economic institutions. The international financial question in the early postwar period was much like that at the end of World War I: on what terms should holders of European currencies be able to buy other currencies, especially the dollar? Should the wartime system of pegged exchange rates and exchange controls be maintained? One concern was that if controls were rapidly eliminated, and a pegged rate maintained, private parties would shift from European currencies into dollars if they could, and the small holdings of gold and dollars of the European central banks would be quickly depleted. The alternative system of floating exchange rates and the rapid elimination of exchange controls was considered unacceptable on the basis of the evaluation of the 1920s experience with floating rates. It was felt that the lack of export capabilities would have led to a rapid depreciation of the European currencies. And so the decision was to maintain the war-time system of pegged exchange rates and exchange controls until European supply capabilities were restored. The use of controls enabled the Europeans to match the size of their payments deficits to the levels of foreign aid—both grants and loans— that they could obtain directly from the United States and indirectly through various international institutions. The maintenance of exchange controls in Europe strengthened the role of the dollar.

By the end of the 1940s, the preeminent international position of the dollar had been firmly established. The United States had the most attractive long-run record in achieving price stability; other countries had experienced rapid inflations, either during or immediately after wars. Several countries had such extensive inflations that they found it necessary to undertake currency reforms and to adopt new currency units. The United States had become the principal international financial center, in regard to the availability of finance, and the financial capabilities of the United States reflected its underlying economic strength.

About ten years later, the dollar appeared weak, not strong. Throughout the 1950s, the United States was almost continuously in payments deficit. U.S. gold holdings were declining, and foreign dollar holdings were rising. While there were periodic assurances that there was "light at the end of the tunnel," the U.S. payments balance did not improve. The U.S. authorities began to lean on their counterparts in other countries to increase their purchases of military and commercial goods in the United

States, to finance more of the local costs of U.S. military troops, and to reduce their barriers to imports from the United States. Monetary authorities abroad were asked not to buy gold from the U.S. Treasury; the dollar was being devalued through the back-door—as a prelude to devaluation through the front door in 1971 and again in 1973.

The Dollar and the Bretton Woods System

The international monetary system of the 1945-1971 period is frequently called the Bretton Woods system, after the New Hampshire resort at which the treaty (the Articles of Agreement) establishing the International Monetary Fund was signed. The Bretton Woods system has been generally viewed as a success, at least until 1971; the evidence cited is the continued growth in world trade and the general world prosperity in the 25 years after World War II, in contrast with the faulty trade and income performance in the comparable period after World War I. The argument is based on the crudest form of causation by association: since the Fund existed and world trade grew rapidly, the Fund was responsible for the rapid growth.

A comparison of the motives for establishing the IMF with the financial developments of the 1950-1970 period is useful in assessing its impact. The rationale for developing a formal set of rules for international financial behavior, which would be incorporated in an international treaty, was to avoid a repetition of the between-wars experience of competitive exchange rate changes and beggar-thy-neighbor employment policies. Rules were needed so that countries would not seek to stimulate domestic employment by increasing their exports relative to their imports, either by devaluing their currencies or by raising their barriers to imports.

The Fund agreement provided an orderly procedure for changing parities; such changes generally required the approval of other IMF members unless the amount of the proposed change was modest. The rules provided that a country could devalue its currency only if it were in fundamental disequilibrium, which meant a nonsustainable payments deficit at its existing exchange parity.

To increase the likelihood that countries would accept this constraint on their future actions, the currencies of its member countries were made available to the Fund, with the view that the Fund could lend these monies to countries with payments deficits and thus reduce their need to change the exchange rates abruptly or to increase their import barriers. The idea was that with more time available for adjustment, unnecessary changes in exchange rates could be avoided. Thus the Fund was a financial intermediary—a conduit by which the national currencies of some member countries could be lent to others following accepted rules. These loan decisions would be made jointly by international civil servants and representatives of member countries, and so the political aspects of these loans would be smaller than those of government-to-government credits.

The Fund agreement also provided that its member countries would reduce and eventually eliminate the use of exchange controls on international payments for goods and services. The Fund had no formal operational powers to compel members to reduce their exchange controls; rather the Fund provided a framework in which the common interests of a group of countries might be brought to bear on those members whose policies violated their commitments.

The central question, in assessing the impact of the Fund over the last 25 years, is whether its members might have acted otherwise in the absence of an agreement. Without doubt, the Fund was effective in inducing member countries to reduce their exchange controls. Whether in the 1950s and the 1960s any member might have followed competitive exchange rate practices of the 1930s, depreciating its own currency excessively so as to improve its domestic employment, is conjectural. The likelihood of such behavior in the postwar period was very low, in part because most of the Atlantic nations were more or less fully employed; none suffered from a massive recession. Indeed the much more usual problem during this period was that IMF members were extremely reluctant to change their currency parities, either to devalue or to revalue, even after a fundamental disequilibrium was evident. And so the post-World War II situation was exactly opposite that of the 1930s: in the earlier period, countries appeared to change their parities too frequently; in the later period, with much too long a delay. The rules suitable for the 1930s were simply inappropriate for the 1960s. One consequence of the reluctance to change parities was that the backdoor approach to balance-of-payments adjustment flourished; deficit countries used a variety of ad hoc controls to limit their payments to foreigners. Surplus countries, in contrast, relaxed these controls to increase their international payments.

Whether the IMF should be held responsible for the stickiness in exchange rates—and in the monetary price of gold—also is conjectural. Yet the availability of IMF loans worked in the direction of increasing the rigidity of the exchange rates, for members were better able to delay changing their parities.

Until the early 1960s, most of the IMF loans involved U.S. dollars, even though the United States was in payments deficit after 1950. The demand for dollars by other members reflected the various international roles of the dollar. And the magnitude of these loans was probably somewhat larger than those the United States might have directly made in the absence of the Fund.[4] In effect, by supplying an international institution with a supply of dollars, the U.S. government made it possible for international civil servants to counsel other Fund members on the appropriate domestic and international economic policies, when political sensitivities about national sovereignty meant that the United States could not counsel these nations directly.

The alternative to the traditional interpretation that the Fund was responsible for the growth of trade and investment is the argument that both world trade and the IMF prospered under the umbrella of a flourishing world economy. The United States felt sufficiently prosperous so that it would not retaliate when other countries pursued trade policies which were discriminatory toward the United States, or when they increased their shares of the markets for particular goods at the cost of U.S. producers. The prosperity, openness, and stability of the U.S. economy made it possible for the Fund arrangement to succeed; it was not adherence to the Fund arrangement that made it possible for U.S. economy or the economies of other Atlantic nations to prosper.

The Bretton Woods system broke down in August 1971 when the U.S. authorities decided to stop buying and selling gold, thus violating U.S. treaty commitments under the Articles of Agreement of the IMF. The shift to a floating rate system and the increase in the number of countries with multiple exchange rates meant that the IMF rules became obsolete. The pace of events was more rapid than the capacity of the Fund mechanism to adjust. The Fund agreement was useful when international financial problems involved payment deficits of other Atlantic countries or of the developing countries; the Fund could lend them money and advise them about appropriate policies. But these arrangements were not designed to cope with the international financial problems associated with world inflation, nor could they deal with an exceedingly large U.S. payments deficit. The economic cause of the breakdown, as opposed to the formal description, reflected the facts that the Fund was coming out from under the U.S. umbrella and that the U.S. authorities were reluctant to receive policy advice from the Fund.[5] That the advice was given suggests a change in the U.S. international financial position. And that the advice was rejected indicates one of the major problems in reforming the international financial system—that of designing rules which apply to the largest country in the system.

Thus in the years before 1971 when the Fund was available, it was not needed to provide order in the international monetary arrangements, although its presence undoubtedly had some impact in facilitating the growth in trade and payments. And when the Fund was needed in the last several years, it proved inadequate; it broke down in its first real test.

III.

The Management of the Dollar-Centered System

The change in the international standing of the U.S. dollar in a span of eight or ten years was dramatic. At the beginning of the 1960s, books were still being written about the "perpetual dollar shortage." U.S. economists were telling each other and anyone else who would listen that the dollar was as good as gold or better; gold was valued at $35 because the U.S. Treasury supported the market at that price. The annual U.S. payments deficits since 1950 were explained by transient phenomena, such as U.S. military expenditures, U.S. foreign aid, U.S. foreign investment, or the foreign demand for dollars.

By the early 1970s, the world was very different. The dollar had been devalued twice by the U.S. authorities, once in December 1971 and again in February 1973, and a third time by investors under the floating exchange rates in the early summer of 1973. Private investors around the world were shifting from assets denominated in dollars to assets denominated in marks, Swiss fancs, and other currencies as well as gold. And central banks in various countries also began to alter the currency composition of their reserve assets, selling dollar assets and buying those denominated in various European currencies. The free market price of gold peaked at over $125 per ounce.

One of the central questions is whether this decline in the standing of the dollar was inevitable, or whether some of these developments were avoidable if the U.S. authorities had followed somewhat different international monetary policies, given their monetary and fiscal policies, as well as the Vietnam War, and their welfare, farm, and security policies. Taking these U.S. policies as givens means that the developments in the real economy would have been largely unchanged; the question is then whether the international standing of the dollar would have been different if the U.S. authorities had taken a different attitude toward their international monetary problem.

Competing Explanations for the Dollar Deficit

The change in the international standing of the dollar is a direct result of the U.S. payments deficit. Each payments imbalance elicits a large number of explanations. Some of the arguments used to explain the dollar shortage were revived to explain the dollar glut. The technological gap had narrowed. U.S. foreign investment was hurting rather than helping the U.S. payments balance. U.S. workers toiled less hard than their counterparts abroad. The United States was more rather than less inflation-prone than Europe. These ad hoc explanations generally involve a crude form of association—e.g., the U.S. payments deficit increased when U.S. foreign aid expenditures increased; therefore the increase in foreign aid "caused" the increase in the deficit.

A more appropriate approach explains the imbalance as a general phenomenon involving the relationships among national economies. Different explanations for the U.S. payments problem are appropriate for particular periods.[6] Three stages can be identified in the dollar problem. One involved the excess demand for dollars; the second, the excess supply of dollars; and the third, the flight from the dollar as a store of value. What needs to be explained, during the first and second stages, is why the U.S. Treasury sold gold and liquid dollar assets to foreign official institutions or why they bought gold and liquid dollar assets. And what needs to be explained in the third period is why investors sold dollar assets, even though, by most measures, the dollar was already undervalued.

The traditional explanation is that the dollar was overvalued, that the prices of U.S. goods and services were too high relative to the prices of comparable foreign goods and services, perhaps because of U.S. inflation at the time of the Korean War or perhaps because of the devaluations of the European currencies in September 1949. Overvaluation of the dollar meant that U.S. goods were noncompetitive in world markets, and U.S. firms had to invest abroad if they were to retain their foreign customers. Overvaluation resulted in payments surpluses for foreign countries as a group, and their purchases of gold and liquid dollar assets reflected how their surpluses were financed.

The nontraditional explanation is that foreign countries as a group wanted to acquire gold and liquid dollar assets, either because continued increases in reserves were necessary before they would feel comfortable in reducing their exchange controls or because higher levels of reserves were necessary to provide the basis for expansion of their domestic money supplies. Because the existing mechanisms for producing international reserves were so inadequate, foreign countries could add to their holdings of gold and of liquid dollar assets only if their currencies were undervalued—if the dollar was overvalued. Hence the nontraditional explanation reverses the causality of the traditional explanation: the driving force is the foreign countries' demand for gold and liquid dollar assets, and the overvaluation of the dollar is the result.

Either theory might be correct. And both explanations are valid, but for different periods. The nontraditional explanation is valid for the 1950-1967 period. Because other countries wanted payments surpluses, the United States had a payments deficit, since payments surpluses and deficits had to be really offsetting. Since the supply of monetary gold was growing less rapidly than the demand, the surplus countries could increase their gold holdings only if some other country would sell gold. Initially the United States was willing to sell gold because U.S. gold holdings at the end of the war had been so high. Many countries wished to add a fiat asset, like interest-bearing time deposits and Treasury Bills, to their holding of reserves. The United States could easily "produce" liquid dollar assets to satisfy this component of the foreign demand for international reserve assets. The sales of both gold and dollars were calculated as part of the U.S. payments deficit, and so the dollar appeared weak in a statistical or accounting sense, even though, paradoxically, it was the strength of the dollar in the international economy that led foreign central banks to acquire dollar assets.

The "proof" of the nontraditional view is that one of the classic signs of overvaluation—more rapidly rising prices in the United States than in other Atlantic nations—was absent. Moreover, none of the surplus countries acted as if its own reserves were too large or increasing at too rapid a rate, at least until the late 1960s. No country complained about the domestic effects of its payments surpluses. No country then behaved like a persistent surplus country and revalued its currency, with the exception of modest revaluations of about 5 percent by Germany and the Netherlands in 1961. Efforts of the United States to reduce its payments deficit by taxing U.S. investors' purchases of foreign investments and the U.S. government's purchases of foreign goods had no demonstrable impact in reducing the U.S. payments deficit, for few other countries would accept the counterpart reductions in their surpluses or the increase in their deficits.

The reason that the United States sold gold and liquid dollar assets to satisfy the needs of others was that the United States was not then willing to be sufficiently harsh in negating the efforts of other countries to achieve surpluses. Nor was the United States willing to adopt bold measures that would enable other countries to satisfy their reserve needs without a U.S. deficit.

The international financial system then seemed stable, or at least it would have seemed stable in the absence of statistics on the U.S. payments deficit. Financing the U.S. deficit led to a progressive weakening of the U.S. reserve position as U.S. gold holdings fell and foreign dollar holdings increased. The ability of the United States to convert foreign-owned dollars into gold on demand was declining.

In about 1967, the nontraditional explanation for the U.S. payments deficit ceased being relevant and the traditional explanation took its place. The approximate cause was the financing of the Vietnam War expenditures on top of the sharply stimulated U.S. economy following the tax cut of 1964. The superheated U.S. economy caused a surge in the U.S. demand for imports: U.S. producers became less interested in exporting. U.S. prices began to rise more rapidly than those in other industrial countries, and U.S. firms responded defensively to the loss of export markets by investing more abroad.

Foreign countries began to acquire more dollar assets than they wanted. Some reduced their import barriers or increased their foreign aid. The countries in Western Europe began to complain of imported inflation as a result of the U.S. deficit, which amounted to $10 billion in 1970. And the U.S. deficit began to grow in 1971. The nontraditional explanation was clearly inadequate; too many countries had payments surpluses larger than they wished.

Other Atlantic nations attempted to insulate their economies from the external consequences of U.S. inflation in various ways. The broad choice was to avoid or sharply dampen their payments surpluses, or to accept the surpluses and neutralize the impact on the size of their money supplies caused by the increase in their holdings of international reserve assets. Some applied exchange controls on the sale of their currency to foreigners; other revalued or allowed their currencies to float. Several attempted to pursue contractive monetary policies to dampen their domestic inflation; their interest rates increased, and they attracted substantial funds from abroad, thus worsening the payments imbalance.

A change in the exchange rates was necessary to restore payments equilibrium. A revaluation of currencies of other Atlantic nations would have resolved the imbalance as would a devaluation of the dollar relative to gold, and hence to their currencies. The economic consequences of both initiatives would have been the same, provided that the resulting exchange rates were similar. But the political consequences differed. The U.S. authorities felt a U.S. initiative would be costly to political support domestically and to the credibility of U.S. international commitments. The governments in other Atlantic nations felt that domestic political costs would be incurred if they took the initiative.

The changes in the exchange rates after 1968 are generally attributed to the U.S. inflation. The revaluation of both the mark and the yen would, however, have been necessary even without U.S. inflation. Both countries developed large payments surpluses as a result of structural change. The traditional exchange rate of 360 yen to the dollar was set in the occupation period to reflect Japan's limited supply capabilities and the unwillingness of the United States to finance large Japanese payments deficits. Similarly, the parity of 4.20 marks to the dollar was set under the occupation, and it prevailed until 1961. Defeat greatly reduced the international competitive power of both Germany and Japan through physical damage, breakdown of established business relationships, and disruption of international commercial ties. But as their economic vigor returned, their supply capabilities increased, they reentered the international economy, and the parities established in the occupation period became obsolete. Initially both countries responded to their growing surpluses by reducing their import barriers and increasing their foreign economic assistance. But as the barriers diminished, the scope for such adjustments declined, and their payments surpluses swelled.

The revaluations of the mark and the yen were an inevitable outcome of the transition of Germany and Japan from occupied countries to full participants in the international economy. Changes in parities of these currencies would have enhanced their attractiveness relative to that of other currencies, including the dollar. But taken alone, the revaluations of two currencies might have seemed too isolated to have reflected adversely on the international standing of the dollar as a superior store of value.

Two Exercises in Hypothetical History

Two exercises in hypothetical history merit attention. The first involves the developments in the dollar's standing if only the factors associated with the nontraditional explanation were relevant. Revaluations of the mark, the yen, and perhaps one or two other currencies would have been necessary even without the Vietnam war and the U.S. inflation. More importantly, an increase in the dollar price of gold—and in the monetary price of gold in terms of every other currency—would have been necessary as U.S. gold holdings fell to the point where the U.S. Treasury would have suspended gold sales. In this sense, while the U.S. inflation advanced the date on which the change in the dollar price of gold was necessary, the advance was perhaps only by several years.

The counterpart exercise in hypothetical history involves assessing the impact of developments in the U.S. international payments position in the post-1967 period if the U.S. international reserve position in 1967 had been that of 1950—that is, if U.S. gold holdings were $25 billion instead of $13 billion, and foreign official holdings of dollar assets were $3 billion instead of $16 billion. Almost certainly changes in exchange rates would still have been necessary to reduce the imbalances associated with the Vietnam inflation, however strong the initial U.S. reserve position. The intriguing question is how substantial the weakening of the U.S. reserve position would have been before the U.S. authorities or those abroad took the initiative in changing the rates. The longer the delay, the weaker the eventual U.S. reserve position. It seems unlikely that the U.S. reserve position would have been worse than it was before the change in exchange rates occurred, and quite possibly it could have been substantially better.

A change in the monetary price of gold was inevitable given the structure of monetary arrangements. The premise of U.S. policy—that the $35 gold parity could be maintained forever—was untenable. And changes in exchange rates were also inevitable given a more rapid inflation in the United States than in other Atlantic nations.

Nevertheless, the U.S. authorities failed to recognize the inevitability of both changes. The U.S. authorities sought to avoid a change in the dollar price of gold by inducing a reduction in the foreign official demand for gold and by developing a fiat substitute for gold. And the U.S. authorities sought to avoid a U.S. initiative in changing the exchange rates. Eventually market forces compelled both changes in the monetary price of gold, and in the exchange rates.

But because of the long delay between the time the need for those changes appeared likely and the time when they occurred, U.S. gold holdings were greatly depleted while foreign monetary authorities acquired an exceedingly large volume of liquid dollar assets. Had the changes in the gold price and in the exchange rates occurred earlier, then distribution of reserve assets would have been less skewed, and the transition to the new monetary arrangements in the next several years easier. Moreover, had these changes occurred earlier, the international standing of the dollar would have declined less sharply and the ability of the U.S. authorities to maintain the initiative in international monetary events would have been enhanced.

The Breakdown of the Smithsonian Agreement

The central feature of the Smithsonian Agreement was a return to pegged exchange rates. The rates embodied in the Agreement were supposed to restore equilibrium, but they did not. Subsequent events have shown them to be short-lived compromises reached through negotiations in an essentially political process. Whether the participants realized then that the resulting exchange rates were inappropriate, but accepted the structure because it was "the best they could get," must remain conjectural. Given the subsequent changes in exchange rates, either the judgments of central bankers about whether to participate in the agreement, or their ability to predict the future equilibrium rates, should be faulted. In the former case, the criticism is that participation in a monetary arrangement likely to break down shortly reduces the credibility of the signatories. And in the latter case, the criticism is that there is high risk in attempting to predict a set of equilibrium exchange rates in a period with sharp divergencies in national rates of price increase.

The crumbling of the exchange rates of the Smithsonian Agreement was piecemeal. First, in June 1972, sterling was floated in response to speculative attacks prompted by the likelihood that a devaluation of sterling would be necessary as Great Britain joined the European Community at the year-end. By the middle of 1972, the yen still seemed undervalued. Speculation in favor of the yen was speculation against the dollar. But the tightness of Japanese exchange controls made it difficult for investors to buy the yen, so instead they bought those European currencies most likely to be revalued along with the yen. A new speculative attack occurred in February 1973: the yen and the European currencies were revalued relative to the dollar, while the dollar was again devalued relative to gold—this time by 10 percent.[7]

Two events in the dollar-mark relationship in 1972 and 1973 also affected the standing of the dollar; both reflect on U.S. policies toward supporting the dollar. When sterling was under pressure in 1972, investors shifted into marks, not because other currencies were weak, but because the mark was more likely to be revalued than the lira or the French franc. The Bank of England sold dollars to support sterling, and the Bundesbank was obliged to buy dollars to prevent the mark from appreciating. The Bundesbank began to be overloaded with dollars. But the prospects of another revaluation of the mark or its shift to a floating currency did not lead to dismay among the U.S. authorities; they wanted speculators to trigger another revaluation of the mark which would improve the international competitive position of the United States. Therefore the U.S. authorities were reluctant to intervene to support the dollar in the exchange market and relieve the pressure on the Bundesbank.

A similar event occurred in early summer of 1973 when the mark was floating. Speculators shifted into marks from the dollar and other currencies, and the appreciation of the mark was self-justifying. Again the authorities in the United States were under pressure to prevent the decline in the foreign exchange value of the dollar. They resisted. So the mark appreciated extensively, perhaps by 20 percent or more above its equilibrium value. That the undervaluation of the dollar might then have improved the competitive position of U.S. goods was a trivial advantage, for the U.S. payments position was not important under the floating system. But the decline in the mark value of the dollar intensified the concern about the stability of the dollar.

The monetary events of the last several years are not independent of those of the previous decade. As a result of the exchange rate changes since 1965, the credibility of central bankers has suffered. These bankers have always been in the position of defending their parities; they were obliged to deny that a change in a parity would occur until it did occur. And so they were usually proved wrong. Over the last five years, investors have learned that there are substantial profits to be made from speculating against weak currencies in favor of strong currencies. In most instances, changes in parities anticipated by investors occurred: in sterling in 1967, in the mark and French franc in 1969 and again in 1971, 1972, and 1973. In contrast, the cases in which a change predicted by investors did not occur were much less numerous; they included the lira in 1963 and the Belgian franc in 1969.

One consequence of the demise of the Smithsonian Agreement was that a system of pegged exchange rates was no longer viable. Investors had lost confidence in the ability of monetary authorities in the Atlantic nations to structure and maintain a system of pegged exchange rates. Investors would not place confidence in new parities until there was once again a demonstration that the commitments of the central banks about parities were credible. This seemed unlikely in a period of world inflation.

A second major consequence of the turmoil in the exchange market has been that the dollar as an international money has been tarnished. The success of an asset as an international money depends on the belief that it will provide a better store of value than competing assets. As other currencies have been revalued relative to the dollar, the dollar's standing as a store-of-value has suffered, for its purchasing power in terms of the revalued currencies has declined.

The standing of the dollar has been affected by the sharp shift in the U.S. approach toward support of the dollar from complete rigidity to total nonsupport. When flexibility was needed to cope with changes in the basic economic relationships involving the monetary price of gold and the exchange rate alignment, it was not forthcoming. And when stability was desirable to cope with destabilizing short-term capital flows, the U.S. authorities took a hands-off attitude. The apparent inability of the U.S. authorities to distinguish changes in basic economic relationships from transient monetary phenomena and tailor their policies accordingly has reduced confidence in the quality of U.S. leadership.

The third consequence of the flight from the dollar has been that the attractiveness of the system of floating exchange rates has diminished. One of the tenets held by advocates of this system—at least before the move to this system in February 1973—has been that speculation would be stabilizing, and that the day-to-day, week-to-week movements in exchange rates would be orderly. The evidence in support of this view was obtained from the Canadian experiences with the floating exchange rates. The experience since February 1973 suggests that the inferences from this experience may not be general. The movement in the dollar-mark rates and the dollar-sterling rates since then cannot be considered orderly. Day-to-day and week-to-week variations in the exchange rate have been substantial in the absence of the steadying impact of central bank intervention.

Yet these movements reflected a shift from the dollar, not because the prices of dollar goods were too high relative to the price of mark goods, but because investors felt they held too large a volume of dollar assets and wanted to diversify their portfolios. So this shift was somewhat self-justifying, since the mark and Swiss franc appreciated. Perhaps these sharp movements might be explained as a transitional phenomena, associated with the shift from a pegged exchange rate system to a floating rate system. But the large movements in the exchange rate also are a response to changes in projections about the differing rates of inflation in the United States and other Atlantic countries.

The monetary events of the early 1970s appear to demonstrate that neither the pegged rate system nor the floating rate system would work. But this conclusion should not be too surprising, for if there is instability in the underlying relationships among national economies, then an exchange rate system is not likely to impose order.

The monetary events of the late 1960s and the early 1970s provide the basis—the set of economic and political experiences, and the web of financial holdings—for international monetary reform. However desirable a return to the Bretton Woods-type of pegged exchange rates might seem, such a return is not feasible until there is a return to relative price level stability. Even then, the lack of credibility about central bank commitments means that such a system would have to provide for more frequent exchange rate changes to cope with speculation.

IV.

Monetary Reform as a Process

For more than a decade, economists, bankers, and government officials have centered much of their time and attention on reform of the international monetary system.[8] Reform has been a subject of multinational negotiations since 1961. In the early 1960s, the attention was on international reserve arrangements: reducing the private demand for gold, strengthening the structure of the International Monetary Fund, and producing a new form of international money. In the late 1960s, attention turned to the exchange rate system—reducing the delays in changing disequilibrium exchange rates.

Currently the core of the monetary reform problem, at least from the point of view of other Atlantic nations, centers on the international roles of the dollar. These countries have pegged their currencies to the dollar and held dollar-denominated assets as part of their international reserves—and they feel abused. The U.S. inflation led to a decline in the real value of their dollar assets (partly offset, however, by the higher interest rates on these assets) and forced them both to revalue and to float their currencies. They trace their domestic price inflations to the U.S. inflation. They now want greater control over their monetary affairs than they believe they have had in the last few years, and they favor monetary arrangements that may help reduce the U.S. impact on their economies.

In considering the path to monetary reform, two factors should be separated. One is the relation of changes in monetary arrangements to the developments in the real economy. The second is the relation between exchange of commitments embodied in any reform arrangement and the consensus among countries on the behavior of the system.

Monetary reform involves the establishment of new institutional arrangements to smooth the financing of trade and investment while enabling countries to obtain greater control over changes in domestic prices and employment. Without reform, trade and investment continue at somewhat greater cost and uncertainty, and perhaps with a marginally smaller growth rate than if there is a new monetary arrangement. Monetary reform can be considered to be a fine-tuning device on an automobile engine—the device may enable the engine to operate at greater efficiency and produce more power, but it cannot cause a two-cycle, two-cylinder engine to become the equivalent of a V-8. So it is that monetary reform cannot really alter the relationships among the various national economies. These relationships are determined by their economic structures: their resource base, their population and labor skills, their capital stock, the relation of their foreign trade sector to their economic structure, and the scope of their financial system.

To suggest that reform cannot have a great impact on the real economy does not mean reform is unimportant. The benefits can be high relative to the costs. And if the agreement can be reached by countries with divergent interests on monetary issues, then this is also likely to create a positive influence on their ability to reach agreement in trade and security issues.

Over time, as the structural relations among national economies change, so international monetary arrangements must also change. Now one of the concerns is whether a new set of arrangements is necessary to recognize the decline in U.S. economic position and the growing economic strength of a united Europe and a resurgent Japan. The evidence for the relative U.S. decline is anecdotal; it includes the more rapid rates of real economic growth in other Atlantic countries, the slowdown in the U.S. technological lead, the deterioration in the quality of

U.S. products, the fragmentation of U.S. society, the disruption in the cities, racial strife, and even Watergate. The devaluations of the dollar are sometimes seen as an indicator of the slippage of the dominant position of the United States. Again the argument involves association rather than causation. Clearly the economic relationships differ from those in 1950 and 1960. The key question is whether these differences are severe or marginal from the perspective of structuring a monetary agreement.

Reform as a Political Process

Despite the attention given to changes in the arrangements for producing international money and for changing exchange rates, relatively little consideration has been given to international monetary reform as a political process. Reform consists of changing the rules that govern the international financial behavior of countries: their practices about exchange market intervention; about loans or credits from the monetary authorities in one country to those in another, arranged either bilaterally or multilaterally through an institution like the IMF; and rules about controls on international payments by the residents of one country to residents of other countries.

Thus the rules of the IMF system obliged member countries to peg their currencies on the exchange market, to follow specified procedures in changing their currency parities, to avoid multiple exchange rate practices, and to limit use of exchange controls on international payments. Moreover, IMF members were obliged to lend specified amounts of their currencies to other members through the IMF and to sell their currencies to the IMF in exchange for gold. Similarly countries that participate in the SDR arrangement are obliged to sell limited amounts of their currencies to other participants in exchange for SDRs. These rules are constraints on a country's actions in the future in that they proscribe it from taking certain actions at some times and oblige it to take other actions at other times. And to say that they are rules means that they are commitments embodied in international treaties or executive agreements.

Monetary reform consists of agreeing to new constraints, or of strengthening the existing constraints on the procedures for changing exchange rates, for lending monies between countries, and for controlling international payments directly. Governments accept these constraints, even though they might compromise their ability to obtain their national objectives, because they believe they gain from having other countries accept similar constraints.

Much of the advantage of the rules derives from increases in certainty about the policies that other countries might take in the future. Thus while each country believes that it might be able to borrow in the future from other countries on an ad hoc basis in the absence of an agreement, if there is an agreement each knows that other countries are obliged to lend specified amounts of their own currencies. Similarly each country might benefit from the commitments that others make about future exchange rate practices. Each country develops a scenario regarding the shocks to which it will be subject in the future as a result of the actions or policies of other countries, and each believes that the shocks may be smaller if the other countries accept specified constraints.

It might seem that each country participating in the negotiations that are part of the reform process would want a set of rules that will constrain the future actions of others with minimum constraints on itself. If any countries seriously followed this position, however, negotiation of an agreement would be virtually impossible. Thus, monetary reform requires a large element of mutuality, at least in a formal sense: each country cannot benefit from the constraints that other countries might accept without in turn accepting similar rules and commitments about its own future actions. Thus the rules of the IMF system were virtually the same for each member.

But to say the rules are the same for each country does not mean that the cost-benefit ratio of accepting a given set of rules is the same for each. Differences in this ratio may result from differences in their economic structures, since some countries have a much larger foreign trade sector than others. Moreover, their economic policies differ; some may be less interested than others in insulating their monetary and fiscal policies from changes in their balance of payments. Or, their attitudes toward a floating exchange rate system or toward changing their currency parities may differ. Finally their attitudes toward unilaterally violating the rules vary.

Monetary agreements tend to embody the consensus. No country with a preference for floating exchange rates had to accept the IMF obligations about pegged rates. But at the time the IMF agreement was negotiated, none had a preference for floating rates. They accepted the commitments because they were convinced of the advantages of pegged rates. On some of the issues involved in the agreement, there may be less than a consensus; smaller countries may participate in the arrangements even though they do not share the consensus, but its success does not depend on their participation. But unless nearly all of the larger countries share the consensus, then an agreement may not be reached.

Even when the agreement has been formulated, each country must be concerned with whether the other participants will adhere to their commitments, especially when doing so might make it more costly for them to achieve their own objectives. Each country questions the credibility of the agreement, and attempts to estimate the circumstances in which it might break down as a result of some countries not abiding by their commitments.

Thus signing a treaty about monetary reform is easier than keeping it. Countries sign treaties because they believe the long-run advantages of adherence to the treaty dominate the short-run costs; the net present value is positive. But each country knows that if the costs of accepting the constraints are too high, then it might ignore its commitments as others might. Consequently the more ambitious the reform incorporated in the agreement—the greater its departure from the consensus and the more rigid the constraints on future actions—the greater the strain that individual countries may incur in honoring their commitments. It therefore becomes more likely that specific commitments will be broken, and thus the credibility of the arrangement is weaker.

In this sense monetary reform cannot get very far in front of the consensus. Almost by definition, an overly ambitious reform arrangement is counterproductive since it is likely to break down; reform is given a bad name. And so the fine issue in proposing reform arrangements involves identifying the extant consensus while shaping the consensus for the future.

Throughout the IMF's history, various members believed that the short-run costs of adhering to their treaty commitments were too high in reference to their national economic objectives. In 1950, for example, Canada adopted a system of floating exchange rates, in effect ignoring the IMF rules. France followed multiple exchange practices in the 1950s. Many countries have maintained exchange controls long after they were committed to their elimination. These violations of the commitments were "accepted" by other IMF members, largely because there were no effective sanctions to use against the offending countires. And most of these violations, especially by the smaller countries, did not threaten the survival of the system. So these countries in effect benefited from the commitments that other countries had accepted at minimal cost to themselves.

The U.S. decision to stop selling gold to foreign central banks was a much more important violation of the Fund Agreement. Other countries then had no incentive to fulfill their commitments.

While the breakdown of the Bretton Woods system highlights the need for a new monetary arrangement, the ability to negotiate new contractual relations has been affected both by the disappearance of the consensus, and by an awareness that any new commitments might break up if it substantially goes against dominant positions of the larger countries. Both factors are important in determining the feasible set of commitments about exchange market arrangements, the arrangements for producing international money, and the future international monetary roles of gold and of foreign-owned dollars.

Reform of the Exchange Rate System

The assumption common to all plans for reforming the exchange rate system, both the ambitious plans and the modest ones, is that each country retains its own central bank and its own currency, and that these central banks pursue monetary policies appropriate for domestic economic objectives. As a consequence, prices will rise more rapidly in some countries than in others, and equilibrium exchange rates—a concept rather than a market reality—will change.

The question for reform involves the rules and mechanisms by which the market exchange rates follow the equilibrium rates. The range of possible exchange market arrangements is small: either currencies float or they are pegged. If they are pegged, the rules for changing the peg must be formulated; the range of options is wide, running from adjustable pegs of the IMF type to crawling pegs of various kinds.

One choice is to institutionalize the floating exchange rate system. Central banks might thereby commit themselves in the extreme never to intervene in the exchange market. Then market forces alone would determine the exchange rates. Alternatively, they might commit themselves to a set of rules indicating when and how monetary authorities in various countries might buy and sell their currencies in the exchange market; the thrust of the rules would be to limit central bank intervention. A different choice involves the adoption of a system of pegged rates; the rules would stipulate when countries cannot change their parities, when their parities must be changed, and when and how they support their currencies in the exchange market on a day-to-day basis in those intervals when the peg is unchanged.

Currently, there is no consensus on the most appropriate exchange rate system and on the scope for flexibility in the exchange rate system. Other Atlantic nations have used a system of floating rates as a second-best choice; they prefer pegged rates and convertibility of their excess dollar holdings into some other reserve asset rather than floating rates and nonconvertibility. The U.S. authorities favor floating rates, at least until they are confident that a pegged rate system will mean that the United States would not again incur payments deficits to supply other countries with part of their reserves, as it did in the 1950-1967 period.

There are, moreover, two other advantages to the floating rate system as viewed by the U.S. authorities. One is that it is more difficult for other countries to keep their currencies undervalued relative to the dollar, as they did in the 1967-1971 period. The second is that exchange market crises—a potential embarrassment to monetary authorities—are less frequent with floating rates than under the pegged rate system. Furthermore, the political costs of a floating rate system, at least the domestic political costs, are likely to be lower than the comparable costs under a system of pegged rates.

That the other Atlantic countries place a higher value on pegged rates reflects two factors. The first is that foreign trade is much more important for their economies than for the U.S. economy: the belief is strong that central bank intervention in the exchange market reduces the uncertainty incurred by those engaged in international trade and investment. And those with this vested interest are relatively more numerous in countries in which foreign trade and investment are relatively large. Moreover, many of these countries have a mercantilist bias; they want to add continually to their holdings of international money, in part for its own sake, and in part because of the stimulus that undervaluation gives to the growth of their export industries.

The return to a pegged rate system is likely to prove difficult, even if there is a consensus. The new system of pegged rates would have to provide for much greater flexibility than is available under the IMF system, primarily because traders and investors have been conditioned to the weaknesses of a pegged rate system, at least as managed in the last decade. The support limits around parity would have to be substantially wider than under the IMF system to discourage short-term capital flows. And changes in pegs would necessarily have to be more frequent.

Monetary Reform and Administrative Regulations of International Payment

One legacy of the Bretton Woods exchange rate system has been a sharp growth in exchange controls on dollar payments abroad—and in other countries, on access to their financial markets. Paradoxically, these controls have probably increased under the floating rate system. Under pegged rates, these controls are adopted to reduce payments imbalances; under floating systems, to reduce the movement in the exchange rate and to isolate national money markets. Such controls represent a bureaucratic response to a payments problem.

Two world wars have led to a massive growth in national bureaucracies. The "bread and butter" of these organizations is administrative regulation; they believe their intervention can improve on the operation of market forces. Frequently, these regulations achieve their impact by imposing costs on foreigners; this is one consequence of the extensive administrative flexibility in designing controls.

Two issues concerning controls arise in the monetary reform process. The first involves the commitments to the controls that are now in effect. The second involves the commitments to the subsequent adoption of exchange controls. The thrust of any commitment in the new monetary arrangement would be to reduce the scope of existing controls and regulate their future use.

Currently, there is no consensus on the use of exchange controls for balance-of-payments adjustment. Other Atlantic nations are more sympathetic to the idea of the use of controls than the U.S. authorities are, at least in principle. In practice, the difference may be small, for the pressure of events forced the U.S. authorities to adopt controls. The concern with exchange controls is not likely to be a major issue in the reform negotiations, for the participants recognize that the commitments can be readily violated without threatening the structure of the arrangement.

Reform of International Monies

One of the central issues in any reform arrangement involves the selection of reserve assets, and the future international monetary roles of gold, the dollar, and of SDRs.[9] One view, although not a dominant one, since the 1940s has been that the international money should be produced by an international central bank, much as a domestic central bank produces a national money. If SDRs were the international money, then national central banks would trade SDRs in the settlement of payments imbalances, much as they have traded gold and dollars. Countries with payments deficits would sell SDRs to the countries with payments surpluses or to the IMF in exchange for a currency to use in exchange market intervention or to repurchase their own currency. The use of gold and the dollar as international monies would be curtailed and phased out, so that eventually SDRs would be the only international money.

There are alternatives to an international arrangement that would have only SDRs as the international money. These include retaining gold and the dollar-denominated assets as international monies, and perhaps using mark-denominated assets or Swiss franc-denominated assets as additional international monies. (The technical problems associated with the transition if the dollar and gold are to be retained as international monies, or if they are to be phased out, are discussed in the final section of this paper.)

One of the central concerns in monetary reform is how to devise a stable numeraire for the system—one that would impart neither the deflationary bias of gold, nor the inflationary bias of the dollar in the 1967-1972 period. The case for the SDR-type arrangement is that the rate of production of international money would be managed, and hence technically, this rate *could* be managed so as to achieve stability in the world price level.

When gold was the numeraire, supposedly there was an automatic mechanism to insure that the rate of production would be varied to achieve world price stability; but this mechanism was ephemeral. In fact, the rate of growth of monetary gold stocks was an historical accident, the residual between gold production and the private demand for gold. The rate of growth of dollar-denominated reserve assets was determined by the decisions of foreign monetary authorities to add to their dollar holdings. The system worked as long as the United States was achieving price stability.

The rate of growth of SDRs will be determined by political factors. Each country will vote in a complicated weighted voting arrangement. It seems almost certain that each country's view on the appropriate rate of growth of SDRs will reflect the impact of each possible growth rate on its ability to achieve its national objectives and to minimize its balance of payments problem. Some countries will favor a rapid rate of growth of SDRs, especially if they believe they are likely to be in payments deficits; they will want to enhance their ability to finance these payments deficits by selling part or all of their allocation of newly-produced SDRs. And they will want to minimize the frequency with which they will have to devalue their currencies. But if these countries have payments deficits then some other countries must have payments surpluses. And the countries that anticipate that they are likely to be in surplus will favor a lower rate of SDR production.

Consequently, the conflict of interest in the rate of growth of SDRs will be sharp. The question of the most appropriate rate of SDR growth from the point of view of stabilizing the world price level would become subordinate to the concern of each country for the impact of each possible rate on its payments position. Indeed, it seems unlikely that any country would give much attention to stabilizing the world price level in determining its preferred rate of SDR growth.

The outcome of this conflict is conjectural. If the rate of growth is rapid, some countries—those with the most conservative domestic monetary policies—may acquire more SDRs than they wish, and so they may revalue their currencies—much as the mark was appreciated relative to the dollar in the last decade. As long as one major country follows a conservative monetary policy so that its currency appreciates relative to SDR, the monetary authorities in other countries will find it in their own self-interest to shift out of SDRs into the assets denominated in the currency of the country with the strongest currency. There would be a shift from SDRs either into other reserve assets denominated in the "strong" currency—if other reserve assets are retained in the system—or into surrogates for reserve assets if direct currency holdings are circumscribed.

Currently, no consensus exists on the move toward an SDR system and on the reduction in the international monetary roles of gold and the dollar. The other Atlantic nations want to retain gold in the system; the United States does not. Retaining gold in a monetary role would require a large increase in the monetary price of gold; without this increase, monetary gold will gradually disappear into private uses and hoards as central banks sell gold in the private market. The United States could increase the monetary price of gold; other countries would quickly follow the U.S. initiative. No other country, however, can unilaterally increase the world price of gold.

There may be more of a consensus about the international monetary roles of the dollar. The U.S. authorities—or at least some U.S. authorities—favor phasing out the dollar as an international reserve asset. They believe its continued role as a reserve asset complicates the attainment of U.S. objectives. The authorities in other Atlantic nations also tend to favor phasing out the dollar as a reserve asset as a way of insulating their own economies from the U.S. economy.

While there appears to be a consensus that the dollar should be phased out as a reserve asset, it is not clear that this position is workable. Central banks and private investors around the world, in seeking to enhance their own interests, must choose from the available assets; given the alternatives, some may still have a preference for dollar-denominated assets. If investors in other countries want to hold dollar-denominated assets, it seems unlikely that U.S. regulations will foreclose this possibility. Moreover, the foreign central banks hold $60 billion of dollar assets, while private parties hold $20 billion of dollar assets. Phasing out the dollar as a reserve asset would mean that the United States would have to repurchase these dollars by selling foreign assets, issuing other U.S. liabilities, or by achieving a payments surplus.

Thus, the consensus on reserve assets is only modestly larger than that on the exchange rate system. National interests diverge, and U.S. priorities toward international monetary reform differ from those of other Atlantic nations. In the absence of a consensus, the scope for monetary reform is limited; any grandiose arrangement would almost certainly falter. For the United States, the issue then becomes whether U.S. interests are served better by muddling through with the ad hoc arrangements, by attempting to secure agreement along the lines of U.S. preferences, or by accepting the preferences of others as a basis for monetary reform.

V.

The U.S. National Interests in International Monetary Reform

The success of monetary reform depends on U.S. initiative and leadership. No proposal for reform can succeed without U.S. agreement; no other country can exercise comparable initiative. Unlike the circumstances of the 1940s, however, the U.S. proposals are no longer accepted as the basis for international monetary arrangements, for the monetary authorities in the other Atlantic countries can as a group prevent the U.S. initiative from being implemented.

Since trade and probably investment have increased in the months since most countries allowed their currencies to float, it must be shown that monetary reform is necessary. The system in effect since February 1973—an arrangement that might be known as the "limping dollar standard"—has been working, and from one U.S. point of view, the system has been reasonably successful. Speculators no longer have the one-way option that they had under the pegged exchange rate system. The dollar is no longer overvalued. Perhaps most importantly, the concern of U.S. monetary authorities with dollar crises is now less pressing, for the costs of the exchange crises have been shifted from their shoulders to those of international traders and investors. Thus the political costs—or more precisely, the domestic political costs—of the U.S. international monetary position have decreased, while the economic costs, which are much more diffuse, may have increased.

That a system of floating exchange rates may seem so attractive is symptomatic of the confusion surrounding the institutional arrangements, and U.S. policy objectives. Floating exchange rates, pegged exchange rates, international central banks, the retention of the $35 parity or the $42 parity, are not the objectives of policy, but rather alternative institutional arrangements under which U.S. policy objectives can be pursued.[10] So specification of the U.S. national policy objectives is necessary to determine the conditions under which particular international monetary reforms would enhance U.S. interests.

The limping dollar standard is a remarkably flexible arrangement, in that each country has a range of options for its exchange rate policy. Some countries peg their currencies to the dollar, much as under the Bretton Woods system. The other Atlantic nations, however, do not; their central banks nevertheless intervene in the exchange market on a discretionary basis, buying or selling dollars as they wish to advance or dampen changes in the dollar value of their currencies. Supposedly, under the limping dollar standard, the U.S. authorities try to be indifferent to the U.S. payments balance, for this balance is no longer a constraint on U.S. policy choices. Similarly the U.S. authorities can supposedly be indifferent to the changes in the foreign exchange value of the dollar, for such changes presently are a response to market forces or the policy decisions of foreign monetary authorities. Both statements, however, ignore the ovjectives of U.S. policy and instead deal with the instruments.

Various costs to U.S. national objectives are incurred by the United States under the limping dollar standard, and some of these costs might be smaller under an alternative arrangement. Some of these costs are economic; some are political and involve the strength of U.S. ties with other Atlantic countries. From the U.S. point of view, monetary reform is worthwhile only if it reduces these costs. And so the costs incurred under the limping dollar standard must be compared with those that would be incurred under one of the alternatives.

The most modest reform involves legitimization of a system of floating exchange rates by which a set of rules would be devised governing central bank intervention in the exchange market. That such a proposal would be accepted seems unlikely, for the other Atlantic nations, having been forced into the second-best (from their viewpoint) situation of a floating rate system, probably would find trivial benefits in accepting constraints on their behavior under this system.

The minimum condition that would have to be satisfied if the other Atlantic countries are to participate in reform requires that the U.S. authorities peg the dollar to an international reserve asset, either gold or SDR. From the U.S. standpoint, one question is whether this commitment to peg the dollar is a constraint on U.S. choices; another is whether the achievement of U.S. objectives would be enhanced by accepting this constraint. Before these questions can be answered, U.S. national economic and political objectives and their relation to various institutional arrangements must be appraised.

U.S. Economic Policy Objectives

Traditionally the statements of U.S. national economic objectives include employment, price level, the growth rate, and perhaps distribution of income—prefaced by suitable adjectives such as high, relative, rapid, and equitable. Since achievement of one objective may conflict with the achievement of one or several other objectives—the employment level or rates of change in price level are good examples—the possible combinations of values for these variables that best satisfies the national interests must be determined.[11]

Once U.S. national economic and political objectives are identified, it is appropriate to consider how the achievement of these objectives is affected by the choice of international monetary arrangements. Do variations in the size of the U.S. payments balance, or in the foreign exchange value of the dollar, or the frequency of U.S. initiatives to change the foreign exchange value of the dollar, have an important impact on the achievement of U.S. employment, price level, growth, or other economic objectives? Is the United States better able to achieve its preferred set of objectives by one of the alternatives to the limping dollar standard; and if so, which one?

The ability of the United States to achieve its national economic and political objectives under the limping dollar standard, which is one without explicit rules, is a useful benchmark for evaluating the possible changes in international monetary arrangements. The first question is whether the differences in the swings in the U.S. payments balance or in the U.S. trade balance that might occur with the shift to an alternative monetary arrangement may have a significant impact on the U.S. employment objectives. Under the pegged exchange rate system, the year-to-year variations in the trade balance are likely to be larger than under the limping dollar standard, since variations in the exchange rate are a substitute for changes in the payments balance. The one reservation is that countries might deliberately undervalue their currencies as a way to stimulate employment in their export industries, and they might do so more effectively in a limping dollar standard world than in a world with rules.

Variations in trade balance are likely to be especially sharp in those industries that are especially sensitive to import competition. In 1971, U.S. imports boomed in automobiles, steel, and electronics; as a result, domestic resources employed in these industries were underutilized. Monetary and fiscal policy were inadequate to deal with these sector-specific problems, especially in the short run; these policies can deal with generalized unemployment problems, but not with those localized in a few industries. Similarly manpower policy may be inadequate to deal with short-run unemployment in a few industries. If participation in a new monetary arrangement limits the size of the variations in the payments balances of other countries, then the U.S. interest may be served, for swings in employment in the few industries that are especially sensitive to imports may be smaller. Hence, a world with rules would enhance the U.S. economic interest if the rules were to limit the swings in the trade balances of other countries.

A second dimension of the U.S. economic objectives involves

the efficient use of resources, which means that lower-cost foreign sources of supply are preferable to higher-cost domestic sources; this may be called the trade-gains effect. International monetary arrangements can be ranked on the basis of the built-in deterrents to trade and investment: the smaller the deterrents, the more desirable the arrangement from the point of view of the efficient use of resources. The greater the frequency of movements in the exchange rate, either under a floating system or under one or another variety of a pegged rate system, the greater the deterrent to trade and investments, and the smaller the gains from trade. Consequently, the greater the stability in the exchange rate, the greater the contribution of international specialization to U.S. domestic income.[12] From this point of view, a system of pegged rates is preferable to the limping dollar standard arrangement—and the less frequently the pegs are changed, the better.

There are trade-offs between employment-stabilization and trade-gains effects. Policies that tend to minimize the variation in domestic employment from swings in the trade balance may be a costly means of maximizing U.S. gains from international specialization. Conversely, policies that maximize efficiency in the use of resources may complicate the attainment of full employment. Ideally, it would be desirable to be able to attach dollar values to the employment and the efficiency aspects and determine how they vary as the monetary arrangements change. In the absence of data on these dollar values, armchair reasoning suggests that the cost to U.S. national income from sacrificing employment to get greater income from the trade-gains effect is probably high relative to the gains.

In the last several years, newspaper columnists have pointed to the revaluations of the mark, the yen, and other foreign currencies as a source of U.S. price increases. They mention two factors. The first is the increased foreign demand for U.S. goods as the price of the dollar declined relative to other currencies. The Japanese demand for U.S. goods has increased because the yen price of the dollar is now much lower. The second is that the decline of the value of the dollar expressed in other currencies has meant that the dollar price of imports has increased, which is sharply evident in the U.S. market for imported automobiles. But the impact of the foreign sector on U.S. price level is relevant to the choice of monetary arrangements only if the price of the dollar would be more likely to fall—assuming changes in the U.S. price level as a given—by a greater extent under some arrangements than under others. And there seems no good reason for believing this decline likely.

One last economic consideration in determining U.S. preferences among alternative monetary arrangements involves *seignorage*—the income that accrues to the producer of money. Thus, if gold is retained as a monetary asset, a substantial volume of resources will be used to mine gold that might otherwise be used in producing dams, roads, and the other productive assets or even consumption goods. To the extent that gold is retained in the system, someone in the system incurs these costs; the United States may share in these costs.

If the dollar is retained as a reserve asset, and foreigners add to their holdings of dollar assets, the United States may gain, since it will be exporting short-term liquid dollar assets; and, in exchange, it will be able to import a larger volume of foreign goods and securities. Similarly if the SDR is a monetary asset and the growth of U.S. holdings of SDRs is smaller than the cumulative allocations of newly produced SDRs, the United States will be able to finance some of its imports of foreign goods and securities with the newly produced SDRs. In contrast, if U.S. SDR holdings exceed U.S. allocations, the United States is somewhat less well off, since it will sell goods and services in exchange for SDRs.

The monetary arrangement that serves U.S. economic interests best is the one that maximizes the benefits of the employment trade-gains effect and U.S. seignorage. Dollar values might be attached to each of these components of U.S. economic interests under the competing arrangements. In general, the dollar values of the employment objective seem likely to dominate those of the other objectives. Specifically, therefore, the system that minimizes swings in the U.S. payments position is more likely to occur in a world with rules than under the limping dollar standard.

The U.S. Foreign Policy Interest and International Monetary Reform

The United States has important foreign policy interests in international monetary reform which are served by signing or accepting international monetary arrangements that will "win friends and influence people" among other governments, even though such arrangements might not be deemed most desirable for U.S. economic interests alone. Thus the U.S. authorities might ask, If the United States were to allow other countries to determine the new international monetary arrangements, would there be substantial economic costs to the United States in variations in the general employment level, the trade-gains effect, or other economic interests?

The U.S. foreign policy interest in international monetary reform is easier to identify than to measure, largely because the interests of various foreign governments differ, and there is no simple way to determine how much weight should be given the interests of each country in determining the "net" U.S. foreign policy interest. The interests of other Atlantic nations differ from those of developing countries (and there are differences among the Atlantic nations themselves) on the future roles of gold and the dollar, on the rate of growth of SDRs and on the distribution of newly produced SDRs among individual countries.

Despite these differences among countries, there are three issues on which they generally agree. Almost unanimously, they agree on the desirability of a return to pegged exchange rates. This preference is inseparably linked to a decision that the dollar again be pegged to an international reserve asset, either gold or the SDR. And they tend to agree on the desirability of reducing the international roles of the dollar. In contrast, they tend to disagree on the future international monetary roles of gold, although it seems likely—judging by their behavior—that a majority of other Atlantic nations favor an increase in the monetary gold price. Taken together, these proposals imply that there should be a limit on the ability of the United States to finance its payments deficits; as the limit is reached, the United States would be obliged to devalue the dollar relative to gold or

SDRs, or to take other measures to reduce the U.S. payments deficit.

Since it seems highly unlikely that the United States would manipulate monetary and fiscal policy so as to improve the U.S. payments position, the U.S. authorities would alter the foreign exchange value of the dollar. This change would incur a variety of costs. There would be modest political costs to the political party in power, since the devaluation is generally associated with unsuccessful economic policies. There would be some foreign policy costs, since the devaluation would be interpreted abroad to mean that the U.S. economy was weak or that it was badly managed. These costs would offset—but only partly—the foreign policy gains from pegging the dollar.

The magnitude of the costs of pegging the dollar would depend on the frequency with which the United States would have to take the initiative in changing the foreign exchange value of the dollar. One of the primary determinants of these changes would be the relationship between the growth in the demand for reserves and the supply of reserves. This issue is more fully discussed in the next section.

Netting the Costs and Benefits of Economic and Political Objectives

If foreign policy considerations were the sole criterion in formulating U.S. policy toward international monetary reform, then the U.S. national interest would be served by pegging the dollar to SDRs or gold; this arrangement would mean that the foreign exchange value of the dollar would also be pegged. The introduction of the various economic considerations complicates the problem. The U.S. interest is served by minimizing the swings in U.S. employment in general and in import-sensitive industries in particular. These swings might be somewhat smaller under a pegged system than if other Atlantic countries were not constrained in the size of their payments surpluses. It is important to develop rules that limit the swings in the national payments imbalances, and it is likely to be easier to get agreement on these rules in the context of an agreement on pegged exchange rates.

Thus, the rules of the system should not permit countries to achieve persistently large surpluses; such countries should be required to revalue. From the U.S. point of view, the new system of pegged exchange rates should not force the United States to devalue the dollar, because the supply and demand for reserves are inconsistent and the United States is the residual supplier of reserves, as it was in the 1950-1966 period. Moreover, when the dollar becomes overvalued, perhaps because U.S. prices are rising more rapidly than prices in other Atlantic countries, the new system should permit the United States to devalue without permitting competitive devaluations by others.

VI.

The U.S. National Interests and Alternative Monetary Arrangements

Economic policy involves choosing among alternatives. The comparisons among alternative proposals for a new monetary system are complex because some arrangements facilitate achieving certain U.S. objectives, while others are better adapted to other objectives. Comparisons of the relative importance of these several objectives are the sort of thing on which reasonable men disagree. Moreover, each of the institutional arrangements has somewhat different implications for the ability of the United States to achieve its objectives when in payments surplus and when in payments deficit; and each of the arrangements has its own implications for the frequency with which the United States is likely to be in surplus or in deficit.

Each reform proposal has a set of implicit benefits and costs for each of the participating countries. Quite possibly, every country might enhance its economic welfare as a result of reform. Some countries may object to particular proposals, either because they anticipate they will be worse off if the proposal is accepted, or because they believe their share of the gains is too small relative to those of other countries.

Two feasibility criteria ease the problem of comparing proposals. First, a proposal is not feasible if it is not consistent with the market forces. Investors are unlikely to hold assets which they believe are likely to decline in value; nor are they likely to forego the opportunity for speculative profits. Central banks, in their selection of reserve assets, are likely to be concerned with the future value of these assets. The second is that any proposal can be considered nonfeasible if it is inconsistent with the preferences of the authorities of other Atlantic countries, on the rationale that they are not likely to accept an arrangement that interferes with their perception of how their interests may be advanced.

There have been numerous proposals for reform of international monetary arrangements over the last decade. But product differentiation has been extensive, and probably excessive, in that there is no measurable economic difference among many of the varieties of gliding bands, floating rates, and crawling pegs, nor among many of the proposals for producing an international money. There are only a few central issues in the realm of international monetary reform; these involve the exchange market arrangements and the number and relationships among reserve assets. Once a position has been taken on these issues, then the details must be left to the government officials who must negotiate the operational implications.

In dealing with the U.S. international monetary reform problem in 1968 (*Choices for the Dollar*), a comparison was made between the costs and benefits to the United States of four monetary arrangements: retention of the $35 parity, raising the dollar price of gold to $42 to correct the U.S. payments deficit, substantially increasing the monetary price of gold to $70 to eliminate the world gold and reserve shortage, and demonetization of gold (the choice of $42 and $70 was symbolic and intended to indicate a type of change, no importance was attached to the amount). The rationale for this set of comparisons was that the United States soon would have to alter the dollar price of gold or else incur substantially higher costs to maintain the $35 parity.

That the dollar price of gold is now $42 might lead to the inference that the U.S. authorities followed one of the alternatives outlined in 1968, and that now one of the current options is the retention of the $42 parity, much as the retention of the $35 parity was in 1968. This inference would be incorrect. There is no effective analogy between the $35 parity and the $42 parity, for the latter is symbolic; the U.S. Treasury has never bought and sold gold at this price, and there is no likelihood that it could ever become an effective parity. And a 20 percent increase in the dollar price of gold, from $42 to $50 (comparable to the increase from $35 to $42 in 1968) as a way to improve the international competitive position of U.S. goods, is unnecessary, for dollar goods are no longer overvalued.

Consequently, only two of the choices available in 1968 are now possible: an increase in the monetary price of gold, perhaps to $90 or $100 an ounce or some other price substantially above the existing parity, or permanent demonetization of gold.[13] There are numerous subsidiary issues, such as the role of dollar-denominated assets as reserves, the future of the $70 billion of U.S. dollar-denominated assets held by foreign central banks, and the exchange market arrangements. But the feasible range of options for these subsidiary issues is narrow.

There is one other major difference from 1968, which involves the rate of inflation. In 1968, the U.S. price indices were less than 10 percent above their 1965 levels; now they are 40 percent above these levels. In 1968, the U.S. inflation was assumed to be a spasm associated with financing the Vietnam War. The spasm metaphor seems no longer appropriate, for the annual rates of price increase have ranged around 5 to 6 percent a year for six years. There is little evidence that this rate will decline. Whether this rate continues or whether relative price stability is attained has a major bearing on the scope for reform.

The institutional arrangements that must be addressed by reform include the rules for exchange market intervention and for the production and ownership of various reserve assets. The SDR is almost certain to have a future role as a reserve asset. While the role of the dollar-denominated assets in the future as reserve assets is uncertain, the implications of the $70 billion of dollar assets held by foreign central banks must be recognized. The role of gold as an international reserve asset is also uncertain; gold will almost certainly be gradually phased out of the system unless there is a substantial increase in the monetary price of gold. Resolving the gold and dollar problems together might be more nearly feasible than resolving them separately.

Monetary Reform: General Principles

Restoring order, stability, and openness to the international monetary system, requires attaining stability in the world price level. Price level stability is the necessary condition for a return to a workable system of pegged exchange rates; without such stability, other Atlantic nations will retain floating exchange rates despite their preference for pegged rates. Pegged rates are not practical in a world in which the relative rates of price increase diverge sharply. In such a world, there is almost certain to be wide variance in the expected rate of price increase in various countries over time. The extrapolation of these rates is likely to show that the equilibrium exchange rates differ from the current spot rates, which will lead investors to shift funds among currencies. The revision of anticipated exchange rates will lead to sharp capital flows and large shifts of reserves among central banks under a pegged exchange rate system; under a floating rate system there will be sharp movements in exchange rates.

The first element in restoring order to the system involves controlling the growth of the numeraire so that a return to relative price stability is possible. The dollar has been the implicit numeraire for 50 years. The SDR may replace the dollar as the formal numeraire, in that various countries may express the parities for their currencies in SDRs rather than in dollars. But it is not clear—the point is largely empirical—that the growth of SDRs could determine the world price level if the United States does not achieve price stability. The rate of growth of SDRs might be set so as to achieve world price stability—although the politics of the decisions regarding the determinants of the growth of SDRs do not point in this direction. But if the rate of growth of the U.S. money supply is substantially more rapid and U.S. prices rise, prices in numerous other countries would rise sympathetically. While some countries might move to a floating rate or revalue their currencies relative to the dollar, their prices might rise along with U.S. prices, although not necessarily by the same amount. If the United States does not achieve price stability, then it seems likely that orderly international arrangements will not be achieved, regardless of the changes in institutional arrangements. U.S. price stability is a necessary prerequisite for monetary reform; without price stability, a new arrangement is likely to prove short-lived.

Even if the U.S. and foreign monetary authorities agree on the desirability of a return to pegged rates, this return should not be immediate, for market exchange rates appear to differ, in some cases extensively, from equilibrium rates. Moreover, because rates of inflation now differ sharply among the Atlantic countries, any set of pegged rates would soon become obsolete and would have to be changed.

Because the credibility of the stability of parities essential to the operation of the pegged exchange rates system has been demolished, the next system of pegged rates must necessarily be quite different from the 1960s version. If relative price stability is the necessary condition, the sufficient condition is that the central banks in the various countries act in such a manner that their statements are credible. When they say that the parities will not change, they must be right. Unless central banks act much more promptly than in the past in changing the parities associated with pegged rates, the new system of pegged rates would be unlikely to last long.

Monetary Reform: The Exchange Rate Mechanism

Flexibility in the exchange rates is necessary as long as central banks in various countries use monetary policies to pursue their national interests. If there is a return to pegged exchange rates, so that rates are not continuously flexible, then flexibility in the pegged rates may be achieved on a discretionary or an automatic basis. The discretionary approach implies that countries are under no international obligation to revalue their currencies—other than bearing the opprobrium of their trading partners—if their payments surpluses are very large. In contrast, the automatic approach requires surplus countries to revalue their currencies if the levels or rates of growth of their reserves are too large.

One may question whether these automatic conditions can be formulated operationally and whether the surplus countries would follow the rules. While the deficit countries might "talk up" the need for the surplus countries to revalue, this approach is counter-productive to stability in the system. Consistency requires that the surplus countries find it in their self-interest to revalue their currencies, and so the rules for changing the exchange rates must match the rules governing growth of reserves.

Certain preconditions must be satisfied if the pegged exchange rate system is to work satisfactorily. The first is that the monetary and fiscal policies in the several countries must be sufficiently similar so that the actual exchange rates do not deviate frequently from the equilibrium rates; changes in the parities of the pegged system are tolerable as long as they are not too frequent. The second is that the authorities must behave so as to maintain their credibility even when changes in parities are necessary. The authorities must minimize the frequency with which they deny that change in the parity will occur and then change the parity. The delays between the time when a change in the parity is necessary and when the parity is actually changed must be minimal so as to reduce the opportunity for profitable speculation against central banks. The third condition is that central banks must have a view of the value of the pegged exchange rate system that transcends their immediate national political advantages.

These conditions were no longer satisfied after 1968. The United States was inflating more rapidly than its trading partners, so that a change in the exchange rates appeared increasingly likely. Yet the authorities continually denied that these changes were necessary; the "light at the end of the tunnel" in resolving the U.S. deficit was always visible to the authorities. Eventually, the need to change the exchange rates became hung up on the political issue of whether the United States or the other Atlantic nations should take the initiative. While the ministers of finance fiddled, speculators earned $5 billion in profits at the expense of national treasuries. The pegged exchange rate system broke down because the authorities were incapable of making it work. They underestimated the speed with which their credibility would decline.

One implicit component of the exchange rate system involves the use of exchange controls and related restraints on international payments. These controls are almost always adopted in lieu of changing a parity. While they are adopted as temporary device, they tend to become institutionalized. Thus virtually all of the restrictions adopted on U.S. payments abroad have been retained. The time to reduce and eliminate these limitations is while currencies are floating, so that market forces can adjust to changes in the equilibrium rates.

The new pegged rate system might be endowed with rules prohibiting the use of such payments-limiting measures in the future. They serve a useful function, however, and it seems more desirable to adopt rules that channel the form and level of payments-limiting measures rather than prohibit them entirely.

In addition to need for consistency between increases in supply of reserves and increase in demand for reserves, consistency is also required between the composition of reserves supplied and the composition of reserves demanded. The reserve mix problem is not directly relevant if the SDR is the only reserve asset—that is, if gold and dollars are demonetized as reserve assets. But both gold and dollars are unlikely to be demonetized.

Monetary Reform: The Future Roles of the Dollar

At the end of 1973, the reserve asset situation was in limbo. While central banks held about $50 billion of gold, its usefulness as a reserve asset was questionable; unless the monetary price was raised, central banks would find it to their advantage to sell gold in commodity markets. Market forces would thus mean that temporary demonetization would become permanent demonetization.

Foreign central banks held $70 billion of U.S. liquid dollar assets, up from $20 billion at the end of 1969. The large increase in their holdings of dollar assets skewed their reserve holdings; they were holding more dollar assets than they wished. One of the central issues is how they move toward an equilibrium position in their dollar holdings; another is how this future equilibrium position is affected if gold is demonetized.

Two issues concern the future roles of the dollar as an international reserve asset. The central one is whether part or all of the $70 billion of dollar assets held by foreign central banks will be funded, consolidated, or converted in SDRs. The second is whether foreign central banks will be allowed to accumulate dollar-denominated assets in the future if they wish to do so. The almost certain answer to the latter question is that if monetary authorities in particular countries find it in their own economic self-interest to acquire dollar-denominated assets, then they will not be constrained from doing so. They must choose among alternative reserve assets, and if dollar-denominated assets appear to satisfy their interests better than assets denominated in other currencies, no U.S. interest would be served by denying them the opportunity to hold dollar assets.

The primary problem deals with the reluctant holders of dollar assets—those who acquired dollar assets, hoping that eventually they might be used to buy gold. If the dollar is pegged to the SDR or gold, some countries may sell dollars and buy these reserve assets, thus reducing the ability of the United States to finance any future deficits from its allocation of newly produced SDRs. The stock aspect of this reserve composition problem should be distinguished from the flow aspect. The stock aspect involves the possible discrepancy between the existing composition of reserve assets, given the level of international reserves, and the preferred composition of reserve assets for this level. The flow aspect of the problem involves the relationship between the preferences of countries for different reserve assets as their reserves increase and the increases in the supplies of various reserve assets. (This distinction may be less clear operationally than it is conceptually, for the adjustment to the stock imbalance occurs over time rather than instantaneously.)

The stock aspect of the reserve composition problem results from the failure of exchange rate and gold price policies in the 1960-1973 period. As a consequence, the dollar holdings of foreign central bank reserves became excessively large. If the dollar is convertible into SDRs or gold, many countries might seek to alter the mix of their reserves to more nearly conform to their preferences—in a sense, to undo the policy failures of the last decade. This adjustment might be made over an extended period, as countries with payments deficits sell dollar assets to finance their imbalances while countries with payments surpluses buy SDRs, or it might be made immediately. In this way, the U.S. holdings of SDRs would be depleted even if the United States is in payments balance—indeed even if it has a payments surplus.

The flow aspect of the reserve composition problem reflects that the composition of reserves demanded each year may not match the composition of the reserves supplied. During the 1950s and the 1960s, the U.S. Treasury sold gold because the monetary demand for gold exceeded the supply available from new production. In the 1970s, the U.S. Treasury might be obliged to sell SDRs, not because the dollar is overvalued, but because the demand for SDRs in many countries might exceed their allocation from new production, and so they would seek to earn SDRs from others.

To protect the United States from an excessive demand for U.S.-owned SDRs, a rule might be adopted that would prevent countries from switching the mix of their reserves, selling dollars and buying other reserve assets. Otherwise the United States might be obliged to change the dollar price of the SDR, not because of a U.S. payments deficit but because foreign countries as a group want to alter the composition of their reserves. Then the foreign exchange value for the dollar that is appropriate to resolve the stock aspect of the reserve mix problem may differ from the foreign exchange value that is appropriate for the flow aspect of this problem. Thus, the dollar might have to be depreciated more extensively so that the United States might earn SDRs in its current trading activities, which it would use to purchase some of the excess dollar holdings from those central banks that wanted to reduce the dollar components of their reserves.

Perhaps a rule might be devised so that the United States would not be obliged to use newly produced SDRs to repurchase excess dollars from foreign central banks; instead the use of SDRs might be limited to finance current U.S. payments deficits. (In this case, dollars acquired by foreign central banks prior to the adoption of this rule would tend to depreciate, implicitly if not explicitly, relative to current deficit dollars.) This rule would mean that no country could alter the mix of its reserves on a marginal basis—it would be obliged to hold the dollar assets. These countries could sell these dollars to finance their payments deficits, but they would be required to rebuild their dollar balances when they were again in payments surplus.

An alternative approach to the reserve composition problem involves consolidation of short-term dollar assets into long-term dollar assets. The rationale is that the United States would be protected from a sudden rush by countries to switch from dollar assets into SDRs. Any country that now wants to buy long-term dollar assets can, so the purpose served by consolidation is unclear. Unless countries are forced to consolidate, the availability of long-term dollar assets does not meet the problem raised by the desire of some countries to sell their dollar assets. And if they are required to hold dollar assets, then the usefulness of consolidation is marginal.

One alternative to devising rules for resolving the flow aspect of the reserve mix problem involves conversion of the excess dollar holdings of various foreign central banks into SDRs.[14] Conversion anticipates the likelihood of shifts from dollars into SDRs by effecting these shifts immediately; thus the U.S. holdings of newly-produced SDRs would not be absorbed in repurchasing the excess dollar holdings of foreign central banks. Countries with a preference for dollars could hold their dollar assets; others however, could switch into SDRs.

Conversion raises one major problem—the impact of an increase in the supply of SDRs, perhaps by a factor of four or five, on the future rate of SDR growth. It seems likely that the larger the volume of dollar assets converted, the slower the rate at which SDRs are likely to be produced each year. The rationale is that the large holders of SDRs will be cautious about the rate of new production so as to reduce the likelihood that the value of their SDRs would decline. Thus one consequence of conversion would be that the flow-supply of SDRs, a politically determined decision, would be low relative to the demand for SDRs; consequently, the United States could find itself facing a demand-determined deficit.

Monetary Reform: The Future Role of Gold

An alternative approach to resolving the stock and the flow aspects of the reserve mix problem is to increase the monetary price of gold. A U.S. initiative to raise the monetary gold price would be followed almost immediately by similar actions of other countries, so that the exchange rates would be largely unchanged. The gold holdings of foreign central banks would increase relative to their holdings of dollars, so the imbalance in the composition of their reserves would decline. And the United States would then be in a better position to sell gold in exchange for foreign-owned dollars, since the monetary value of U.S. gold holdings would be larger.

The virtue of gold in the monetary system is not that it is some kind of basic or fundamental money, endowed with mystical properties. Rather, its advantage is that it is a useful kind of international money with a long history of acceptance.

An increase in the monetary price of gold also eases the balance of payments adjustment problem—the flow aspect of the reserve mix problem. At a higher gold price, the commodity and hoarding demand for gold would be smaller, gold output would be larger, and so monetary gold stocks would increase. It is possible that every country could add to its gold holdings simultaneously; indeed every country could have a payments surplus at the same time. There is a monetary price of gold at which the United States would neither buy or sell it; at higher monetary prices, its gold holdings would increase. To the extent that those countries with large dollar holdings—holdings they now believe too large—could add to their gold holdings each year from new production, they would feel less pressure to quickly unload their dollar assets.

The monetary price of gold that may be appropriate for a solution to the stock aspect of the reserve composition problem may not be appropriate for a solution to the flow aspect of this problem. The stock aspect of the gold problem involves setting the monetary price of gold such that, given the levels and compositions of reserves, and the preferences among reserve assets, the individual countries are on balance satisfied with the existing composition of reserve assets after the increase in the monetary gold price and the subsequent adjustments. They would no longer feel their dollar holdings too large, for the value of their gold holdings would have increased while the value of their dollar holdings would remain unchanged. The flow aspect of the problem involves setting the monetary price of gold such that increases in the monetary demand could be satisfied without forcing the United States to sell gold—not because of a U.S. payments deficit, but because of the shortage of monetary gold.

The monetary gold price appropriate for resolving the stock aspect of the reserve mix problem may be too high or too low to resolve the flow aspect of the reserve mix problem. The implication of a monetary gold price that is too high to resolve the flow aspect of the problem is that the United States would buy gold, since the amount of gold available for monetary holdings would increase more rapidly than the demand of other countries for gold. In contrast, if the monetary price of gold is too low, the amount of gold available for monetary holdings would increase less rapidly than the demand of other countries for gold, foreign official institutions would buy gold from the United States, and U.S. gold holdings would decline. Eventually an increase in the monetary price of gold would again be necessary. In contrast, if the price of gold is too high, the United States incurs the costs of acquiring too much gold. This cost is the yield on the assets the United States otherwise would have acquired if it had not imported gold.

Deciding on the appropriate monetary price of gold is necessarily a crude calculation. Thus, it is appropriate to determine the costs that are incurred if the monetary price is too low and if it is too high. If the monetary price is too low, U.S. holdings of gold and SDRs would decline. Alternatively, if the monetary price is too high, the United States would accumulate more gold and SDRs than it would prefer. Thus, the cost of an error from too high a price must be weighed against the cost of too low a price; costs of an error on the high side seem smaller than one of the same percentage amount on the low side.

An increase in the monetary gold price provides a solution that consolidation and conversion do not, because, at the higher gold price, foreign official institutions would be holding more dollar assets because they would be holding more gold. In effect, the ability of the United States to determine the monetary price of gold means that Gresham's Law operates in favor of the dollar rather than against the dollar.

Thus if the dollar is again to be pegged to an international reserve asset, the U.S. national interest is enhanced if gold is retained as a reserve asset, even though an increase in the monetary gold price is required. Ironically, one reason why an increase in the monetary gold price is advantageous is that it redresses the imbalances resulting from the delays in changing the exchange rates in the years before 1971.

Epilogue

The design and negotiation of new monetary arrangements that promise to realize order, stability, and openness encounter numerous constraints, so that the set of feasible choices is small. One of the constraints is that these arrangements must be tied to the underlying real economy—to the size and economic power of various national economies, and to preferences of central banks in different countries for particular reserve assets and for certain approaches toward adjustment to payments imbalances. No arrangement will prove workable unless it is consistent with the structure of the world economy. Another constraint is that the $50 billion of central bank holdings of monetary gold and the $70 billion of their U.S. dollar assets cannot be phased out as reserves without severe repercussions on the adequacy of the domestic monetary base in individual countries and on the adequacy of international reserves. A further constraint is that individual nations are willing to put only limited trust in the commitments made by other nations; signing a treaty does not automatically increase the credibility of the arrangements.

These constraints suggest that it would be difficult—but not impossible—to develop an alternative to the limping dollar standard that would bring net economic gain to the United States. Under this standard, the movements in the exchange rates in several currencies have been quite large, so that trade and investment patterns have been distorted. Moreover, within several countries pressures toward central bank intervention in the market have been strong; such pressures are likely to increase, perhaps quite rapidly, should there be recessions. Consequently, the likelihood of competitive exchange rate depreciation would be high if several of the larger countries were to undergo recessions at the same time, for there are no formal rules to constrain such behavior. And so, there is some urgency in the U.S. initiative to reestablish a set of rules for central bank behavior in the exchange market, even before the reduction in the U.S. inflation rate makes it feasible to return to pegged rates.

The comparison of net gains to the United States from participating in an alternative to the limping dollar standard suggests that the U.S. foreign policy interest may be enhanced, at least in the short run, by agreeing to an international arrangement leading to a modified, pegged exchange rate system. But whether the U.S. foreign policy interest is served in the long run depends on whether the United States is likely to find itself in sharp disagreement with other countries—both about which countries should take the initiative in changing exchange parities, and about the rate of growth of international reserve assets.

One element in negotiations leading toward a new international system has involved efforts of other Atlantic countries to reduce their susceptibility to shocks from the United States by developing an SDR-centered system; the dollar would then lose its international roles. The United States would have an important voice in managing the system, as would the other large Atlantic countries. But because national interests diverge, collective management of the international system may not succeed in resolving the conflicts over how adjustments to imbalances should occur. The politics of the Atlantic community appear too diffuse to permit development of money produced by an international institution at the center of the system; the divergence in economic interests may be too sharp to permit reconciliation at the political level. The result of this effort to enhance order and stability might be a substantial decline in openness and in the freedom for international transactions.

One of the major U.S. concerns, before accepting the commitments embodied in new arrangements, must be their implications for the position of the dollar relative to gold and the SDR. U.S. authorities must be convinced that accepting the commitment to convert dollars owned by foreign central banks into other reserve assets will not lead to an excessive drain on U.S. reserve holdings, either because the increase in the demand for reserve assets exceeds the increase in the supply, or because some foreign central banks wish to reduce their holdings of dollars and increase their holdings of other reserve assets.

The alternative approach toward a new system involves moving toward a more decentralized system within the framework of a higher monetary price for gold. This system would provide scope for each country to hold the preferred mix of its reserve assets; each could hold its desired combination of gold, dollars, and SDRs. The dollar could again be convertible into gold and SDRs; the overhang problem would be resolved. Within this framework, finance ministers could deescalate their almost continual negotiations on how to resolve evolving international finanacial problems.

International monetary problems will remain even if the United States again achieves price stability and there is a return to pegged exchange rates under the umbrella of a higher monetary price of gold. No single agreement can be signed that will eliminate monetary problems any more than the U.S. Constitution eliminated U.S. political problems. International financial problems are inevitable as long as there are nation-states and national monies. What is needed is a set of arrangements that minimizes the scar tissue generated in the process of resolving these disputes among the Atlantic nations.

NOTES

1. Henry James once said, "When I say Oxford, I mean Oxford and Cambridge." In this sense, the term "Atlantic nations" includes Japan and Australia, as well as the industrial nations of Western Europe and Canada. With respect to some aspects of the problems, it might be more appropriate to say "Japan," and implicitly include the European nations.

2. Descriptions of the system are available in numerous sources. One of my "favorites" is R. Z. Aliber (1973a), especially chapters 2 and 3.

3. Assume Germany holds $5 billion in gold and $5 billion in dollar-denominated assets when the exchange parity is 5 marks to the dollar and the gold parity for the dollar is $35. At these exchange rates the gold holdings of Germany are valued at 25 billion DM, and their dollar holdings at 25 billion DM. Assume both the Germans and Americans are convinced that the mark should be revalued to 4 marks to the dollar. If the Germans take the initiative and revalue the mark in terms of the dollar and gold, then German gold holdings are valued at 20 billion DM. If, instead, the United States takes the initiative and the dollar price of gold is increased to $42 and the mark price of gold is unchanged, the mark value of German gold reserves becomes 24 billion DM while the mark value of its dollar holdings becomes 20 billion DM.

4. The companion Bretton Woods institution, the International Bank for Reconstruction and Development (the World Bank) initially was supposed to be used to finance reconstruction in Europe. It did make a few loans of dollars, and in this sense there is a close parallel to the IMF. But it quickly became evident that the Bank's resources were hopelessly inadequate for financing postwar reconstruction, and so the Bank was shelved when Marshall Plan aid became available.

5. Sometime before August 1971, Pierre-Paul Schweitzer, who was then the Managing Director of the International Monetary Fund, recommended that the United States raise the dollar price of gold as a way to effect a change in the exchange rate structure. The United States did not find the advice compatible with its own policies, and the U.S. government opposed Schweitzer's reelection to a third term as Managing Director.

6. For most of the 53 years since 1920 the United States has been in payments deficit—except during wars and other periods of substantial political uncertainty.

7. In early February, Congressman Wilbur Mills made a public statement indicating the need for a change in the exchange rate structure, thus inviting speculation against the dollar. In August 1971, Congressman Henry Reuss had made a similar statement on the need for a change in the exchange rate structure, with similar consequences.

8. This section on monetary reform as a process is an extension of the argument developed in R. Z. Aliber (1973b).

9. The term SDR is used generically to include the various international monies that might be produced by the IMF or an institution like the IMF.

10. This confusion between the objectives of policy and the instruments of policy is only one of the errors in the formation of U.S. international monetary policy. Another has been the inability to understand the nature of the foreign official demand for gold.

11. As long as the number of targets does not exceed the number of instruments, it is technically feasible to achieve all of the objectives. But what is technically possible may not be institutionally or politically feasible.

12. Businessmen complain that floating exchange rates complicate their international transactions. They have reason to complain, for floating rates shift uncertainty from central bankers to corporate treasurers.

13. The use of a price range of $90 to $100 rather than $70 reflects the fact that the commodity prices are about 40 percent higher than in 1968—but these prices are suggestive rather than precise.

14. In addition to consolidation and conversion, there is a third possibility: evaporation. Central banks that hold these dollars would "write them off" in a sort of reserve Marshall Plan. This proposal is silly; it is hard to see how the European interest would be served. And it is presumptuous of Americans to offer this advice to other governments as being in their interests.

15. This argument is developed more fully in R. Z. Aliber (1973b: 13-17).

REFERENCES

ALIBER, R. Z. (1973a) The International Money Game. New York: Basic Books.

——— (1973b) "National preferences and the scope for international monetary reform." Princeton University Essays in International Finance 101 (November).

——— (1969) Choices for the Dollar. Washington, D.C.: National Planning Association.

——— (1966) The Future of the Dollar as An International Currency. New York: Praeger.